THOUGHTS WITHOUT
A THINKER

THOUGHTS
WITHOUT A
THINKER

PSYCHOTHERAPY
FROM A
BUDDHIST PERSPECTIVE

Mark Epstein, M.D.

BasicBooks
A Division of HarperCollinsPublishers

Parts of chapter 5 previously appeared in different form in *Tricycle: The Buddhist Review* as "Freud and Dr. Buddha: In Search of Selflessness." *Tricycle* 1, no. 3 (spring 1992).

Copyright © 1995 by Mark Epstein, M.D.
Published by BasicBooks, A Division of HarperCollinsPublishers, Inc.

Designed by Ellen Levine

Library of Congress Cataloging-in-Publication Data
Epstein, Mark, 1953–
    Thoughts without a thinker: psychotherapy from a Buddhist perspective / Mark Epstein.
      p. cm.
    Includes index.
    ISBN 0–465–03931–6
    1. Buddhism—Psychology.   2. Psychotherapy—Religious aspects—Buddhism. 3. Meditation—Buddhism. I. Title.
    BQ4570.P76E67 1995
    616.89'14'0882943—dc20   94–38063
                                              CIP

95 96 97 98 ◆/HC 9 8 7 6 5 4 3 2 1

MAY – 3 1995

For Arlene

It has been put rather differently by Pirandello as the title of a play—Six Characters in Search of an Author. *But why stop at that? Why should it not be something which is even smaller, more fragmentary than that? It is a thought wandering around for some thinker to lodge itself in.* —W. R. Bion

Contents

Foreword by the Dalai Lama   ix

Acknowledgments   xi

Introduction: *Knocking on Buddha's Door*   1

PART I
THE BUDDHA'S PSYCHOLOGY OF MIND

Chapter 1   The Wheel of Life: A Buddhist Model of
            the Neurotic Mind   15

Chapter 2   Humiliation: The Buddha's First Truth   43

Chapter 3   Thirst: The Buddha's Second Truth   59

Chapter 4   Release: The Buddha's Third Truth   75

Chapter 5   Nowhere Standing: The Buddha's
            Fourth Truth   89

PART II
MEDITATION

Chapter 6   Bare Attention   109

Chapter 7   The Psychodynamics of Meditation   129

PART III
THERAPY

Chapter 8	Remembering	163
Chapter 9	Repeating	181
Chapter 10	Working Through	203
Notes		223
Index		235

Foreword by the Dalai Lama

THE PURPOSE OF LIFE is to be happy. As a Buddhist I have found that one's own mental attitude is the most influential factor in working toward that goal. In order to change conditions outside ourselves, whether they concern the environment or relations with others, we must first change within ourselves. Inner peace is the key. In that state of mind you can face difficulties with calm and reason, while keeping your inner happiness. The Buddhist teachings of love, kindness, and tolerance, the conduct of nonviolence, and the theory that all things are relative, as well as a variety of techniques for calming the mind, are sources of that inner peace.

Recently, psychotherapists, with their background in science and medicine, have begun to explore the possibilities of employing Buddhist techniques in a therapeutic context. I feel this is entirely consistent with the aim of overcoming suffering and improving the welfare of all sentient beings. Living experience of Buddhist meditation has given practitioners a profound knowledge of the workings and nature of the mind, an inner science to complement our understanding of the physical world. On its own no amount of technological development can lead to lasting happiness. What is almost always missing is a corresponding inner development. This is an area in which there is increasing evidence that Buddhist assertions and modern findings have the potential to be valuable to one another.

I am greatly encouraged to see these approaches develop. I congratulate Mark Epstein on completing this book, the result of twenty years' experience in both Western psychotherapy and Buddhist meditation. *Thoughts without a Thinker* will not only offer useful insights to therapists, but also stimulate further study and mutual cooperation between therapists and followers of the meditative path.

December 1994

Acknowledgments

A s I PUT THIS BOOK together, I was struck by the number of teachers I have had who had nothing to do with my orthodox schooling or training. This comes from someone who has spent the better part of his life in some kind of educational facility. It is to the credit of those institutions that I still had the time and energy to explore outside the established venues. I thank only a fraction of those who made a difference for me, those who most directly influenced my writing of this book.

For his kindness, generosity, and indefatigable wisdom, I would like to thank the late Isadore From, who patiently guided me through my first years as a psychotherapist. I wish he were still here. For their meditation instruction, guidance, and example, I am fortunate to be able to thank Jack Kornfield and Joseph Goldstein. For teaching, encouragement, and discussion over the past twenty years, all of which have figured into this book, I am indebted to Daniel Goleman. For reaching out to me and revealing the life that yet flourishes in psychoanalysis, I am grateful to Emmanuel Ghent, Michael Eigen, and Gerald Fogel. In addition, Helen Tworkov, Jack Engler, Stuart Margulies, Mark Finn, Karen Hopenwasser, Bob and Nena Thurman, Richard Barsky, Anne Edelstein, Scott Martino, and my editor, Jo Ann Miller, have all contributed to my efforts to bring together the often disparate worlds of Buddhism and psychotherapy. Arlene, Sonia, Will, and the rest of my family gave me the peace of mind that I needed to carry this project to completion, while my patients have inspired me with their openness, honesty, and humor. I would like to thank them each by name, but will refrain.

My patients have generously shared themselves with me and provided material for this book; in all cases cited herein I have changed names, as well as other identifying details, or constructed composites, in order to protect privacy.

THOUGHTS WITHOUT
A THINKER

KNOCKING ON
BUDDHA'S DOOR

THE QUESTION I am most frequently asked has to do with how Buddhism has influenced me as a therapist, how I have integrated it into my work. This is a formidable question, since I did not set out to become a "Buddhist psychotherapist." I pursued a study of both Eastern and Western systems simultaneously. I met my first meditation teachers at about the same time that I was exposed to Freudian theory, traveled to India and Southeast Asia around the time of my medical studies, and spent weeks in silent retreat before ever sitting with my first therapy patient. I was not schooled in how to integrate the two: I had no real choice in the matter. As befits the intensely personal nature of both meditation and psychotherapy, my own attempts at integration have been, above all, private ones.

This is a far cry from the way in which the great psychologist William James imagined it would be. James was impressed with the psychological sophistication of Buddhism and predicted that it would be a major influence on Western psychology. A story about him sets the stage for this book. While lecturing at Harvard in the early 1900s, James suddenly stopped when he recognized a visiting Buddhist monk from Sri

Lanka in his audience. "Take my chair," he is reported to have said. "You are better equipped to lecture on psychology than I. This is the psychology everybody will be studying twenty-five years from now."[1] James was one of the first to appreciate the psychological dimension of Buddhist thought, yet he was not as accomplished at prophecy as he was at psychology. Several years earlier, in Vienna, Freud had published *The Interpretation of Dreams*, and it was Freud's psychology, not the Buddha's, that has had a far greater impact in the West over the subsequent decades.

At the time of James's lecture, the influence of Eastern philosophy was just beginning to be felt among Western psychologists. In psychoanalytic circles, an interest in Oriental thought was common. Many of Freud's early colleagues and followers (including Ernest Jones, Otto Rank, Sandor Ferenczi, Franz Alexander, Lou Andreas-Salome, and Carl Jung) were conversant with ideas about Eastern mysticism and attempted to address it from a psychoanalytic perspective. Freud's friend Romain Rolland, the French poet and author, was a devout follower of the Hindu teachers Ramakrishna and Vivekananda, and he engaged Freud in a lively correspondence about his meditative experiences, as described extensively in Freud's *Civilization and Its Discontents*. Fascinated by, if somewhat skeptical of, his friend's reports, Freud struggled to apply his psychoanalytic understanding to Rolland's experiences. In 1930 Freud wrote:

> I shall now try with your guidance to penetrate into the Indian jungle from which until now an uncertain blending of Hellenic love of proportion, Jewish sobriety, and philistine timidity have kept me away. I really ought to have tackled it earlier, for the plants of this soil shouldn't be alien to me; I have dug to certain depths for their roots. But it isn't easy to pass beyond the limits of one's nature.[2]

As one who shares with Freud all three of these characteristics—the "love of proportion, Jewish sobriety, and philistine timidity"—I can attest that none of them need make the Buddhist approach incomprehensible. Freud himself did his best to penetrate the Indian jungle, despite his misgivings. Under Rolland's influence, Freud described the "oceanic feeling" as the prototypical mystical experience: a sense of limitless and unbounded oneness with the universe that seeks the "restoration of limitless narcissism" and the "resurrection of infantile helplessness."[3] This equation of the meditative experience with a return to the breast or the womb has gone virtually unchallenged within the psychoanalytic community since Freud's commentary. While it does capture some truth, it takes no account of the investigative or analytical practices most distinctive of Buddhism and most related to the psychodynamic approach. Whereas James seemed to be opening psychology up to the potential contributions of the Buddhist approach, Freud effectively closed it down. This stemmed not from Freud's unwillingness to apply psychoanalytic investigation to the range of meditative states but from a basic unfamiliarity with what Buddhist meditation, at least, was actually about.

James understood something that subsequent generations of more psychoanalytically influenced commentators did not: the essential *psychological* dimension of Buddhist spiritual experience. Far from being a mystical retreat from the complexities of mental and emotional experience, the Buddhist approach requires that *all* of the psyche be subject to meditative awareness. It is here that the overlap with what has come to be called psychotherapy is most obvious. Meditation is not world denying; the slowing down that it requires is in service of closer examination of the day-to-day mind. This examination is, by definition, psychological. Its object is to question the true nature of the self and to end the production of self-created mental suffering. It is a pursuit that various schools of psychotherapy have been approaching independently, often without benefit of the overarching methodology of the Buddhist psychologists of mind. As long as Buddhism could be seen as a mystical, or otherworldly, pursuit, as an Eastern exoticism incomprehensible to the Western mind, as a spiritual pursuit with little relevance to our complicated neurotic attachments, it could be kept isolated from the psychological mainstream, and its insights could be relegated to the esoteric shelves of "Eastern philosophy." Yet, Buddhism has something essential to teach contemporary psychotherapists: it long ago perfected a technique of confronting and uprooting human narcissism, a goal that Western psychotherapy has only recently begun even to contemplate.

Slowly and steadily, especially since the late 1960s and the 1970s, Eastern thought has crept into the psychological consciousness of the West. Fueled by Jung's break with Freud, by the Beat poets' embrace of Zen in the 1950s, and by the counterculture's linking of psychedelia and Eastern mysticism in the 1960s, the psychological dimension of Eastern thought has labored under the stamp of "alternative" since its first infiltration of the West. The influence of Eastern thought may be seen in the work of the psychologist Abraham Maslow and in the development of the humanistic branch of modern psychology, and several psychoanalytic pioneers (notably, Erich Fromm and Karen Horney) were attracted to Buddhist thought late in their careers. Nevertheless, the worlds of Eastern thought and mainstream Western psychoanalysis have remained remarkably insulated from each other over the years. While Freud's concepts have become dominant, completely taking over the language of psychology, and while psychoanalysis has continued to evolve as a forum for exploring the nature of psychological experience, virtually none of the modern popularizers of Buddhism in the

West—whether translators, authors, or teachers—have been fluent in the language of psychoanalysis. In presenting the Eastern approach, they have generally stayed outside the scope of psychodynamic psychotherapy, enabling the more traditional psychotherapists to continue to ignore them.

Fed by the early contributions of James, Jung, Aldous Huxley, Alan Watts, Thomas Merton, and Joseph Campbell, the broad outlines of Asian thought have been painted for the Western mind. Stressing the universality of "cosmic consciousness" or mysticism in all religions, these authors did much to popularize a notion of a "perennial philosophy" common to all spiritual traditions. These early explorers of Eastern thought recognized the uniquely psychological nature of the Buddhist texts that were available to them, but they did not often distinguish the Buddhist approach from any of the others. They tended also to downplay the specifically Buddhist techniques of analytic inquiry into the nature of self that are so relevant for today's psychotherapists. They were generalists who synthesized a great deal of disparate information and translated it into a necessarily simplified form that could be digested by an audience for whom all of this information was new. However, few of these early translators had extensive training in the meditation practices that distinguish Buddhism from other Eastern approaches. And, although they respected the psychological clarity of the Buddhist teachings, their relative inexperience with both clinical psychotherapy and with intensive Buddhist meditation has hampered the development of an effective integration of the two.

In the meantime, as psychotherapy has grown in scope and sophistication over the years, its parallels with Buddhist thought have become ever more apparent. As the emphasis in therapy has moved from conflicts over sexual and aggressive strivings, for instance, to a focus on how patients are uncomfortable with themselves because, in some fundamental way, they do not know who they are, the question of the *self* has emerged as the common focus of Buddhism and psychoanalysis. While the Western tradition has grown quite adept at describing what has been called the narcissistic dilemma—the sense of falseness or emptiness that propels people either to idealize or to devalue themselves and others—much controversy has arisen over the psychoanalytic method's applicability for such problems. In fact, Western therapists are in the position of having identified a potent source of neurotic misery without having developed a foolproof treatment for it. In reaching this point, many within the field of psychology have finally caught up to James: they are ready to look at the psychological teachings of the Buddha.

Buddhist psychology, after all, takes this core sense of identity confusion as its starting point and further claims that all of the usual efforts to achieve solidity, certainty, or security are ultimately doomed. It not only describes the struggle to find a "true self" in terms that have impressed Western psychologists for decades (some of Freud's inner circle studied newly translated Buddhist texts for the insights they shed on narcissism), but also offers a *method* of analytic inquiry unavailable in the Western tradition. From the Buddhist perspective, meditation is indispensable to free the individual from neurotic misery. Psychotherapy may be equally necessary, especially to expose and reduce erotic or aggressive conflict, but the psychotherapeutic dialogue will always come up against the problem of the restless and insecure self. Psychotherapy can identify the problem, bring it out, point out some of the childhood deficiencies that contributed to its development, and help diminish the ways in which erotic and aggressive strivings become intertwined with the search for a satisfying feeling of self, but it has not been able to deliver freedom from narcissistic craving.

Freud showed signs of recognizing this deficiency late in his life in his paper "Analysis Terminable or Interminable,"[4] and generations of therapists and patients alike have had to settle for the relative relief that psychotherapy has had to offer. Buddhism clearly promises more, and because of this promise, it has caught the attention of the psychotherapeutic community, primed, as it has been, by the "discovery" of narcissism. This book represents the outcome of my own struggle to reconcile the teachings of the Buddha with the insights of Western psychology, the two principle influences on my own development.

People are attracted to the Buddhist approach, but it remains enigmatic; they know that it speaks to them, yet they have trouble translating the message into a form applicable to their daily lives. Still approached as something exotic, foreign, and therefore alien, the power of the Buddhist approach has not really been tapped, and its message has not yet been integrated. The situation is analogous to that of China two thousand years ago, when Taoism was the prevailing philosophy and Buddhism was first introduced. It was up to those Taoist scholars who also became adept at Buddhist meditation to accomplish the "Sinification" of Buddhism, producing a new hybrid—Chinese Buddhism, or Zen. In our culture, it is the language of psychoanalysis, developed by Freud and carefully nurtured by generations of psychotherapists over the past century, that has seeped into general public awareness. It is in this language that the insights of the Buddha must be presented to Westerners.

With this in mind, I have organized my book into three parts, entitled, respectively, "The Buddha's Psychology of Mind," "Meditation," and "Therapy." Part I is designed to introduce the Buddha's psychological teachings in the language of Western psychodynamics. I do this not only for the benefit of those in the fields of psychology or psychotherapy but also for those attracted to Buddhist philosophy or meditation who, nevertheless, have only a sketchy idea of the Buddhist approach's conceptual basis. Part I is meant as an orientation to the Buddhist perspective, since we in the West have already spawned a number of misconceptions about the basic teachings of the Buddha. Filled with psychological ideas derived from Freudian theory and struggling with psychological issues that are often incompletely resolved or not even addressed, Westerners engaged in meditation practice all too often are derailed by their own longings, conflicts, and confusion. In describing the Buddha's psychology in Western psychological language, I hope to combat that unfortunate trend.

Part II, "Meditation," is meant to explain the basic Buddhist attentional strategy of *bare attention* and to show how the meditative path may be understood in psychodynamic terms. By presenting the psychological underpinnings of traditional practice, I hope to make clear how relevant these ancient techniques still are for the Western mind. The meditative practices of bare attention, concentration, mindfulness, and analytic inquiry speak to issues that are at the forefront of contemporary psychodynamic concern; they are not about seeking some otherworldly abode. By showing how these meditative experiences may be understood in psychological terms, I hope to make clear how potent a force they can be in conjunction with more traditional Western psychotherapies.

Part III, "Therapy," takes Freud's treatise on the practice of psychotherapy, "Remembering, Repeating and Working-Through," and uses it as a template for considering how the Buddha's teachings can be integrated into the practice of psychotherapy. These chapters spring directly from my own experiences as a meditator, patient, and psychotherapist, in which the two worlds of Buddhism and psychotherapy have not always been so distinct. I was in the relatively unusual position of learning about Buddhism *before* I became a psychiatrist, and

I studied meditation before either entering or practicing psychotherapy. In fact, my introduction to Buddhism came in classes at Harvard University in the psychology building called William James Hall, where, fifty years later than he had predicted, James's prophecy was beginning to take root. In part III, I try to show how the practice of Buddhism has infiltrated my own clinical work; how the Buddha's teachings might effectively complement, inform, or energize the practice of contemporary psychotherapy; and how many of today's most important clinical psychotherapists have been, often unknowingly, knocking on Buddha's door.

I begin with a discussion of what has always impressed me the most about Buddhist psychology: its comprehensive view of the human psyche. For Buddhism, like the Western traditions that followed many centuries later, is, in its psychological form, a *depth* psychology. It is able to describe, in terms that would make any psychoanalyst proud, the full range of the human emotional experience. Although he may not have shared any of Freud's three defining traits of "love of proportion, Jewish sobriety, or philistine timidity," the Buddha may well have been the original psychoanalyst, or, at least, the first to use the mode of analytic inquiry that Freud was later to codify and develop. In the traditional description of the Wheel of Life and, again, in the teachings of the Four Noble Truths, we find the fruits of this analytic investigation. As the title of this book, drawn from the English psychoanalyst W. R. Bion, is meant to imply, the Buddha's teachings are not necessarily at odds with the psychodynamic approach. Sometimes, in fact, they are just what the doctor might order.

PART I

THE BUDDHA'S PSYCHOLOGY OF MIND

The mind that does not understand is the Buddha: there is no other.

—D. T. Suzuki

A FALSE START

IN THE EARLY days of my interest in Buddhism and psychology, I was given a particularly vivid demonstration of how difficult it was going to be to forge an integration between the two. Some friends of mine had arranged for an encounter between two prominent visiting Buddhist teachers at the house of a Harvard University psychology professor. These were teachers from two distinctly different Buddhist traditions who had never met and whose traditions had in fact had very little contact over the past thousand years. Before the worlds of Buddhism and Western psychology could come together, the various strands of Buddhism would have to encounter one another. We were to witness the first such dialogue.

The teachers, seventy-year-old Kalu Rinpoche of Tibet, a veteran of years of solitary retreat, and the Zen master Seung Sahn, the first Korean Zen master to teach in the United States, were to test each other's understanding of the Buddha's teachings for the benefit of the onlooking Western students. This was to be a high form of what was being called *dharma* combat (the clashing of great minds sharpened by years of study and meditation), and we were waiting with all the anticipation that such a historic encounter deserved. The two monks entered with swirling robes—maroon and yellow for the Tibetan, austere gray and black for the Korean—and were followed by retinues of younger monks and translators with shaven heads. They settled onto cushions in the familiar cross-legged positions, and the host made it clear that the younger Zen master was to begin. The Tibetan lama sat very still, fingering a wooden rosary (*mala*) with one hand while murmuring, *"Om mane padme hum,"* continuously under his breath. The Zen master, who was already gaining renown for his method of hurling questions at his students until they were forced to admit their ignorance and then bellowing, "Keep that don't-know mind!" at them, reached deep inside his robes and drew out an orange. "What is this?" he demanded of the lama. "What is this?" This was a typical opening question, and we could feel him ready to pounce on whatever response he was given.

The Tibetan sat quietly fingering his mala and made no move to respond.

"What is this?" the Zen master insisted, holding the orange up to the Tibetan's nose.

Kalu Rinpoche bent very slowly to the Tibetan monk next to him who was serving as the translator, and they whispered back and forth for several minutes. Finally the translator addressed the room: "Rinpoche says, 'What is the matter with him? Don't they have oranges where he comes from?'"

The dialogue progressed no further.

CHAPTER I

THE WHEEL OF LIFE: A BUDDHIST MODEL OF THE NEUROTIC MIND

A S DIFFICULT as it was to find common ground between the two Buddhist masters, it is far more daunting to seek congruence between the psychological traditions of East and West. For me, though, the Buddhist picture of the Wheel of Life (Wheel of Samsara), one of the most ubiquitous images of the Buddhist world, has always seemed a particularly useful starting place in comparing Buddhist and Western notions of suffering and psychological health. The Wheel of Life depicts what are known as the Six Realms of Existence, through which sentient beings are said to cycle endlessly in their round of rebirths. In artwork, this circular form, or *mandala*, is set into the yawning jaws of Yama, the lord of death. The mandala vividly illustrates all six of the realms to which beings are subject: the Human Realm, the Animal Realm, the Hell Realm, the Realm of the *Pretas* (Hungry Ghosts), the Realm of the *Asuras* (Jealous Gods or Titans), and the God Realm. These are the major subdivisions, and texts on the subject describe hundreds of realms within each. Leading off of the wheel, emerging out of the Human Realm, is a path to Buddhahood, signifying the special opportunity implicit in the human birth: the realization of Buddha-mind, an awakening that leads to escape from the Wheel of Life.

The Wheel of Life is used in Buddhist countries to teach about the concept of *karma* (merit), the notion that a person's actions in this life will affect the kind of rebirth he or she will take in the next. Harming others contributes to rebirth in Hell Realms; indulging the passions, to rebirth in Animal Realms; giving to others (and especially to monks or monasteries), to more comfortable human births or rebirths in God Realms, and so on. The actual psychological teachings about karma are much more sophisticated than this, of course, but the mandala is the kind of image that children or beginners can grasp easily. The essential point is that as long as beings are driven by greed, hatred, and delusion—forces represented in the center of the circle by a pig, a snake, and a rooster attempting to devour one another—they will remain ignorant of their own Buddha-nature; ignorant of the transitory, insubstantial, and unsatisfactory nature of the world; and bound to the Wheel of Life.

Yet, one of the most compelling things about the Buddhist view of suffering is the notion, inherent in the Wheel of Life image, that *the causes of suffering are also the means of release*; that is, the sufferer's perspective determines whether a given realm is a vehicle for awakening or for bondage. Conditioned by the forces of attachment, aversion, and delusion, our faulty perceptions of the realms—not the realms themselves—cause suffering. Inset into each realm is a tiny Buddha figure (actually, a representation of the Bodhisattva of Compassion, an enlightened being whose energy is devoted to the eradication of suffering in others), who symbolically teaches us how to correct the misperceptions that distort each dimension and perpetuate suffering. We do not experience any of the realms with clarity, teach the Buddhists; instead, we cycle through all of them fearfully, cut off from a full experience, unable to fully embrace them and afraid of what we will see. Just as the thoughts in our minds keep endlessly chattering as if beyond our control, so we slip from realm to realm without really knowing where we are. We are locked into our minds, but we do not really know them. We are adrift and struggling, buffeted by the waves of our minds, having not learned how to float.

This is the other way to understand the Wheel of Life, to take it less literally and more psychologically. The core question of Buddhist practice, after all, is the psychological one of "Who am I?" Investigating this question requires exploration of the entire wheel. Each realm becomes not so much a specific place but rather a metaphor for a different psychological state, with the entire wheel becoming a representation of neurotic suffering.

According to Buddhism, it is our fear at experiencing ourselves directly that creates suffering. This has always seemed very much in keeping with Freud's views. As Freud put it, the patient

> must find the courage to direct his attention to the phenomena of his illness. His illness itself must no longer seem to him contemptible, but must become an enemy worthy of his mettle, a piece of his personality, which has solid ground for its existence and out of which things of value for his future life have to be derived. The way is thus paved for the reconciliation with the repressed material which is coming to expression in his symptoms, while at the same time place is found for a certain tolerance for the state of being ill.[1]

This belief that reconciliation can lead to release is fundamental to the Buddhist notion of the six realms. We cannot find our enlightened minds while continuing to be estranged from our neurotic ones. As Freud so presciently remarked, "When all is said and done, it is impossible to destroy anyone *in absentia* or *in effigie*."[2] In each realm of our experience, teach the Buddhists, we must learn how to see clearly. Only then can the suffering that the Buddha identified as universal be transformed. Release from the Wheel of Life, from the Six Realms of Existence, is traditionally described as nirvana and is symbolized by the path leading off of the Human Realm. Yet it has become a fundamental axiom of Buddhist thought that nirvana *is* samsara—that there is no separate Buddha realm apart from worldly existence, that release from suffering is won through a change in perception, not through a migration to some kind of heavenly abode.

Western psychology has done much to illuminate the six realms. Freud and his followers insisted on exposing the animal nature of the passions; the Hell-ish nature of paranoid, aggressive, and anxiety states; and the insatiable longing of what came to be called oral craving (which is depicted in pictures of the Hungry Ghosts). Later developments in psychotherapy brought even the upper realms into focus. Humanistic psychotherapy emphasized the "peak experiences" of the God Realms; ego psychology, behaviorism, and cognitive therapy cultivated the competitive and efficient ego seen in the Realm of the Jealous Gods; and the psychology of narcissism was specifically about the questions of identity so essential to the Human Realm. Each of these trends in psychotherapy was concerned with returning a missing piece of the human experience, restoring a bit of the neurotic mind from which we had become estranged.

This concern with repossessing or reclaiming all aspects of the self is fundamental to the Buddhist notion of the six realms. We are estranged not just from these aspects of our character, the Buddhist teachings assert, but also from our own Buddha-nature, from our own enlightened minds. We have

ample opportunity to practice the methods of re-possessing or
re-membering that are specifically taught in meditation, for we
can practice on all of the material of the six realms, on all of the
sticking points in our minds.

If aspects of the person remain undigested—cut off, denied,
projected, rejected, indulged, or otherwise unassimilated—they
become the points around which the core forces of greed, hatred,
and delusion attach themselves. They are black holes that
absorb fear and create the defensive posture of the isolated self,
unable to make satisfying contact with others or with the world.
As Wilhelm Reich demonstrated in his groundbreaking work
on the formation of character, the personality is built on these
points of self-estrangement; the paradox is that what we take to
be so real, our *selves*, is constructed out of a reaction against just
what we do not wish to acknowledge. We tense up around that
which we are denying, and we experience ourselves through our
tensions. One recent patient of mine, for example, realized that
he had developed an identity centered on feelings of shame,
unworthiness, and anger rooted in a momentary experience of
his mother's emotional unavailability when he was a young
child. Sensing her absence, he had become afraid, but this fear
was too threatening to his psyche so he instead converted it into
feelings of inadequacy, making himself the problem. It was not
until many years into his adulthood when his mother lay paralyzed by a stroke and was physically unable to respond to him
that he could finally acknowledge his fear. The fabric of self is
stitched together out of just these holes in our emotional experience. When those aspects that have been unconsciously refused
are returned, when they are made conscious, accepted, tolerated,
or integrated, the self can then be at one, the need to maintain
the self-conscious edifice disappears, and the force of compassion
is automatically unleashed. Only when my patient was finally

able to acknowledge his own fear at his mother's emotional unavailability could he begin to feel sympathy for *her* emotional predicament. His shame had prevented that beforehand. As the famous Zen master Dogen has said:

> To study Buddhism is to study the self.
> To study the self is to forget the self.
> To forget the self is to be one with others.

Through the teachings of the Wheel of Life we are reminded that it is not enough to expose the inhibitions in just one or two of the six realms; we must do so in all. A person who is cut off from his passions but not from his God-like nature will be as unbalanced and insufferable as a person who suffers from the reverse scenario. Many of the movements in Western psychotherapy have gone very deeply into the sufferings of one particular realm, but none have explored the entire wheel. For example, Freud explored the Animal, or Desire, Realm; the child analyst Melanie Klein, the Hell Realm of anxiety and aggression; the British psychoanalyst D. W. Winnicott and the developer of self-psychology Heinz Kohut, the Human Realm of narcissism; and the humanistic psychologists Carl Rogers and Abraham Maslow, the God Realm of peak experiences. All of these approaches have been helpful—indeed, essential—for the treatment of particular sticking points, but they are inherently limiting because each one focuses exclusively on only one dimension. To one degree or another each may well be necessary, but the Buddhist tradition sees the entire mandala as reflective of the neurotic mind, and it therefore requires an approach that can be applied comprehensively.

Within the wheel, the Buddhist technicians of mind emphasize the special opportunity inherent in the Human Realm, out of which the path to liberation is drawn. It is from this realm that the essential meditation technique of *bare attention* emerges; this strategy undergirds most of the effective therapies developed for each of the other realms. The Human Realm suffuses all of the others, then: it is the linchpin of the wheel, the domain of Narcissus, in search of himself and captured by his own reflection.

With this in mind, let us look more closely at each of the Buddhist realms and the struggles within them. I would like to start with a personal story.

THE HELL REALM

When my daughter was three years old, right around the time that her brother was born, she developed a pronounced fear of the wind. At first we excused it—the wind can be quite strong and gusty coming off the Hudson River in lower Manhattan, and she still seemed so small. We went out of our way to reassure her and shield her, but her fear only grew more intense, and my wife and I began to react with a start ourselves whenever a breeze came up. Other children reacted calmly when the wind blew, but we were huddling in doorways, darting for cover, wrapping each other in layers of protective clothing, and otherwise becoming completely dominated by this burgeoning dread. My daughter was steadily slipping into a Hell Realm, howling with fear at the merest touch of a breeze. She was afraid, she said, either that she would be swept away by the wind, deposited in the sea, and then eaten by a giant whale, or that the wind was going to get inside her and blow her up.

In the Tibetan paintings of the Wheel of Life, beings in Hell Realms are depicted as suffering an assortment of infernal tortures. They can be seen boiling in hot oil, being dismembered by wild animals, freezing, starving, and suffering a variety of other hideous punishments. Being tortured by the wind is not one of the most common, but there was no question about the Hell-ish nature of my daughter's experience. From a psychodynamic perspective, the Hell Realms are vivid descriptions of aggressive and anxiety states; beings are seen *burning* with rage or *tortured* by anxiety. They do not recognize their torturers as products of their own minds, however. They believe themselves to be tortured by outside forces over which they have no control. At the same time that they are completely dominated by their rage or anxiety, they are cut off from those same emotions. They do not see that those unwanted forces are their own, and they are therefore imprisoned in a cell of their own making. The Bodhisattva of Compassion is sometimes inset into the Hell Realm holding a mirror or a purifying flame, indicating that this suffering can only be alleviated by seeing the unwanted emotions in the mirror. When so recognized, the emotions themselves become healing (a point that was not lost on Freud).

A good six months after the flowering of my daughter's phobia, after a summer vacation spent cowering indoors, we sought an outside consultation. The wind had come to represent an intolerable feeling of my daughter's, which she had projected from inside of her to the outside world. What could have been so intolerable? Certainly, we recognized that her brother's birth had had some impact on her, and we were alert to the well-known possibility of sibling rivalry. But she seemed genuinely fond of him, caring and protective, and showed a minimum of hostility toward him. Our attempts at sensitivity to her anger toward her brother had, however, obscured the real picture. Her feelings toward her brother were not creating conflict, but her feelings toward her mother were. It was her rage at the very person whom she so loved and

needed that was so intolerable and that we had missed in the
face of her apparently loving acceptance of her new brother.

She was furious at her mother, it turned out, but these feelings were so strong and so dangerous that they could not be
owned without our help. She had done the best she could without us, protecting us from her rage by eliminating it and taking on the consequences herself. Once we realized the problem,
it resolved with incredible speed. My wife engaged my daughter in play that was allowed to develop into a kind of play
fighting. My daughter needed little encouragement once she
saw that this was not forbidden, and very soon they both col-
lapsed on the floor, laughing, crying, embracing, and pummel-
ing each other. The fear of the wind diminished as my daughter regained her fighting spirit, and for a while we encouraged
her to shadow box with the wind or yell at it or race into it. As
she came to see that we could tolerate her fury, that her anger
at the loss of an exclusive relationship with her mother was
understandable, the phobia disappeared. She looks back on the
episode now, five years later, with nothing but amusement.

There is a parallel in the legends that surround the transmission of Buddhism from India to Tibet, said to be first accomplished by the great Indian yogi Padma Sambhava in the
eighth century. Tibet at that time was dominated by a shaman-
istic tradition, and Tibetans were deeply superstitious and fearful of the many spirits and magical forces felt to be lurking in
the outside world. Padma Sambhava, it is told, engaged the
best shamans of the indigenous Bon religion in a competition
in which he proved his magic powers to be superior, beating
them at their own game. In the process, he is said to have
defeated the powerful animal-headed demons of the lower
realms and converted them to protectors of Buddhism, revealing their true natures as aspects of the enlightened mind rather
than as demonic forces. The Tibetan tradition has since been

replete with images of such beings "stomping on the corpse of ego," representing the harnessing of painful emotion and the progression from projection, paranoia, and fear to integration and clear vision.

When we refuse to acknowledge the presence of unwanted feelings, we are as bound to them as when we give ourselves over to them indignantly and self-righteously. Religion has traditionally counseled believers to withdraw from aggressive, erotic, or egotistical states of mind, replacing them with the "purer" states of devotion, humility, or piety. Psychoanalysis has encouraged its adherents to be less fearful of these emotions, to understand their roots and recover the energy that has been lost through the failure to accept primitive urges or longings. Buddhism, alone among the world's religions, has taken a characteristically middle path, recognizing the need to be free from destructive emotions while at the same time seeing that such freedom comes through nonjudgmental awareness of just those emotions from which we seek freedom.

As the Hell Realm seems primarily associated with states of fear and aggression, the contributions of Winnicott on the necessity of hate in the growing child may be instructive in illustrating the attitude that the Buddhists encourage toward such feelings. Winnicott sees the infant as possessing a natural urge to be at one with that which she loves, seeking to destroy the mother's separateness with a ruthlessness and singlemindedness that any woman who has nursed her children will attest to. He developed the concept of the "good enough mother" who could manage this attack without being destroyed, who could survive the assault without withdrawing in horror, retaliating with fury, or otherwise abdicating her maternal presence.[3] Part of this "good enough" response is also to resist the destruction perpetrated by the child, to stand her ground, set limits, define a boundary, and thereby induce some element of frustration into the baby's experience. The other part of the good enough response is to permit the rage, to accept the rupture that it heralds. This facilitates the maturation of the child from a state that Winnicott calls "object relating" to one of "object usage"; that is, from a state in which the mother is experienced as nothing but an extension of the infant to one in which the mother's separateness is grasped.

The child's hatred and aggressive urges, when properly met and "held" by the mother, force a destruction of the infant's own outmoded ways of relating. When improperly met, the child's rage knows no bounds, and she becomes relegated to a Hell-ish existence. As Winnicott implies, failures in this sphere often bring people into psychotherapy or propel them into meditation. One of the contributions of the Buddhist approach is its ability to teach a method of relating to one's own rage that is the psychic equivalent of Winnicott's "holding."

THE ANIMAL REALM

The Animal Realm is the realm of instinctual gratification, of the biological drives of hunger and sexuality. In the Tibetan cosmology, its distinctive characteristic is stupidity. The Bodhisattva image inset into this dimension is shown holding a book, which represents the capacity for thought, speech, and reflection that is lacking in our animal natures. Such an image may also represent the idea of sublimation that Freud was to develop out of his own exploration of these instincts, drives, or urges.

Freud's explanations dovetail with the Buddhists' in the realization that ultimate happiness cannot be derived from sensual pleasures. There are inherent limitations to the pleasures of sexual gratification, Freud found. By mining the nature of sexuality, he came to the paradoxical conclusion that there is "something in the nature of the sexual instinct itself [that] is unfavorable to the realization of complete satisfaction."[4] Rather than unleashing a never-ending torrent of unregulated passion, as many sexually conflicted persons fear, integration of the Animal Realm inevitably reveals pleasure to be inherently fleeting. It cannot be sustained forever, we find, and its completion returns us to a state of impoverishment, of unrest, of separateness, desire, or tension. Freud's description of pleasure elucidates a basic Buddhist concept, namely, that the pursuit of pleasurable sensory experiences leads inevitably to a state of dissatisfaction, because it is in the nature of pleasure not to be sustainable:

> What we call happiness in the strict sense comes from the (preferably sudden) satisfaction of needs which have been dammed up to a high degree, and it is from its nature only possible as a periodic phenomenon. When any situation that is desired by the pleasure principle is prolonged it only produces a feeling of mild contentment. We are so made that we can derive intense enjoyment only from a contrast and very little from a state of things. Thus our possibilities of happiness are already restricted by our constitution.[5]

Although sexual pleasure has become much more accepted since Freud's time, the inhibitions around freedom and happiness in sexuality have certainly not disappeared. They have perhaps been complemented by an attitude of indulgence, by an attempt to extract lasting pleasure or meaning from what is essentially a transient pleasure, but the inhibitions described by Freud persist, at least for some people. In fact, some who develop an interest in Buddhism have a tendency to try to escape from unresolved sexual issues through meditation, but this usually works only for a time. The more likely scenario is that the sexual issues become more pressing because of the spiritual work.

A number of my patients with extensive meditation experience have come into therapy after discovering unavoidable sexual issues through their practices. One woman, after spending years on retreat in India, found she could no longer avoid the truth of her homosexuality. Her biggest fear was of disappointing her homophobic and fragile parents, whom she knew would take the news as a reflection of their own "failings." Another patient, raised in a strictly Catholic Korean home, came into therapy after several intensive retreats emphasizing to me one too many times that he could take or leave sex, that he felt no urgency, not even a strong desire for orgasm when having sex. Beneath these claims lay his desire to integrate his sexuality and his fears that such an integration was impossible, that his animal nature would overwhelm him if he gave it a chance. Like the patients with trouble integrating their anger, he tended to see his sexuality as an "it," as something separate that threatened the rest of him. At one point in the therapy he had a dream of his family's church being invaded and overwhelmed by dancing and drinking heathen revelers. At another point, he regaled me with stories about a recent trip to a sadomasochism parlor where he had experimented with various kinds of domination. He wanted to show me, he said, just how dangerous it was going to be for him to unleash his passions, just how far his erotic imagination could take him. Once he became less embarrassed about his erotic yearnings, however, they began to take their natural place, and unencumbered by them, he was able to proceed with his spiritual work and his life. Paradoxically, looking at the Animal Realm was the only way for him not to be stuck there. This is a lesson that many spiritual groups of both East and West have had to learn over and over again. Ignoring the Animal Realm only seems to empower it, as the sexual scandals that have rocked spiritual groups and leaders testify. Sexuality is a threat to spirituality only when it is not integrated.

While the Animal Realm cannot be ignored, it *can* be put in its place. Sexuality certainly does not require the indulgence that is often associated with it, but it does not have to be separated from the enlightened mind. Indeed, the Tibetan tradition makes liberal use of copulation as a metaphor for the enlightened mind, and advanced Tantric meditation practices, which are taught to monks after years of preparation in order to catalyze an awakening, often culminate in a ritualized act of sexual intercourse.

THE REALM
OF THE HUNGRY GHOSTS

The Hungry Ghosts are probably the most vividly drawn metaphors in the Wheel of Life. Phantomlike creatures with withered limbs, grossly bloated bellies, and long, thin necks, the Hungry Ghosts in many ways represent a fusion of rage and desire. Tormented by unfulfilled cravings and insatiably demanding of impossible satisfactions, the Hungry Ghosts are searching for gratification for old unfulfilled needs whose time has passed. They are beings who have uncovered a terrible emptiness within themselves, who cannot see the impossibility of correcting something that has already happened. Their ghostlike state represents their attachment to the past.

In addition, these beings, while impossibly hungry and thirsty, cannot drink or eat without causing themselves terrible pain or indigestion. The very attempts to satisfy themselves cause more pain. Their long, thin throats are so narrow and raw that swallowing produces unbearable burning and irritation. Their bloated bellies are in turn unable to digest nourishment; attempts at gratification only yield a more intense hunger and craving. These are beings who cannot take in a present-day, albeit transitory, satisfaction. They remain obsessed with the fantasy of achieving complete release from the pain of their past and are stubbornly unaware that their desire is fantasy. It is this knowledge that such people are estranged from, for their fantasy must be owned as fantasy. The Hungry Ghosts must come in contact with the ghostlike nature of their own longings.

This is not an easy thing for a hungry ghost to accomplish, however, even with the help of a psychotherapist. Indeed, the problems of the Realm of the Hungry Ghosts are increasingly turning up in psychotherapists' offices. A recent patient of mine, for example, an accomplished teacher of French literature named Tara, personified the predicament of the hungry ghost. Describing a long succession of relationships with other accomplished academics at the top of their fields, Tara repeatedly developed an impassioned relationship with one such man while already involved with another. Invariably, she kept the man whom she was actually living with at bay. She would quickly and critically uncover all of his faults, lose interest in him sexually, and essentially prevent him from touching her, either physically or emotionally. At the same time, she would begin to fantasize about the next luminary to enter her life. While very experienced sexually, she rarely reached orgasm and confessed to a vague discomfort with sexual intimacy. She remembered an unhappy and critical mother who had rarely touched her as a child and who had once, in a fit of pique, ripped up and destroyed Tara's teddy bear, because of Tara's obstinacy. Tara came to therapy after first trying to practice Zen meditation (*zazen*), which she found herself inexplicably terrified of, to the point of having to bolt from the meditation hall (*zendo*) in lieu of sitting with herself.

Tara was searching insatiably for the kind of nourishment that she had once needed but that was now inappropriate to who she was as an adult woman. (Even if she could have found someone to hold her as her mother never had, it is unlikely that this would have been satisfying for very long. Instead, such behaviors would have seemed suffocating, being no longer relevant to her adult needs.) She feared what she also most desired (being touched) and was unable to experience the transitory satisfactions available to her. The possibility of a relationship with one man only stimulated a resurgent fantasy of a liberating relationship with another, and Tara could not see that as an unreachable fantasy. Indeed, she was very resistant to even discussing these fantasies. She was driven by them but unable to acknowledge their reality, let alone their unreality. It was only when she began to be able to articulate her yearnings that she could feel the pain of her mother's treatment of her. At this point, her fear of zazen began to diminish, and her compulsive need to denigrate those who sought intimacy with her began to become conscious.

In the traditional depiction of the Wheel of Life, the Bodhisattva of Compassion appears in the Realm of the Hungry Ghosts carrying a bowl filled with objects symbolic of spiritual nourishment. The message is clear: Food and drink will not satisfy the unfulfilled needs of this realm. Only the nonjudgmental awareness perfected by the Buddha offers relief.

This desperate longing for inexhaustible abundance is very common in the Western psyche, where it masquerades under the heading of "low self-esteem." It is a mind state that has, paradoxically, proved difficult for many Eastern Buddhist teachers to understand in their Western students. The extent of inner feelings of emptiness and unworthiness in the Western psyche has seemed all but unbelievable to teachers raised in the East, and the compelling fantasies of reparation that are often attached to those same teachers are rarely dealt with in any kind of thorough psychoanalytic fashion. Just as the emptiness of the Hungry Ghosts must be experienced in such a way that reparation is no longer sought from impossible sources, so the Western student afflicted with such feelings must make the emptiness itself the object of his or her meditation. Only then can self-loathing be transformed into wisdom, a task in which both psychotherapy and meditation may well collaborate.

THE GOD REALM

In the Buddhist cosmology, the Heaven Realms are places of sensual bliss and gratification, of rapture and aesthetic pleasures. They are inhabited by beings with subtle bodies, not prone to illness, who delight in music and dance and exist in extended versions of what has come to be called peak experiences, in which the participant dissolves into the experience of pleasure, merging with the beloved and temporarily eradicating the ego boundaries. This is the state that has been called confluence in Gestalt therapy: the merger of orgasm, the assimilation of digested food, the attunement of the infant at the breast, the satisfaction of any completed experience in which a new whole is created and the self temporarily dissolves. Such experiences are powerful states, cultivated in Buddhist practices but also warned against in Buddhist teachings, because of their ability to induce complacency with what remains at base a temporary interruption or refuge. The Bodhisattva of Compassion appears in the God Realm holding a lute, thus signifying the musical pleasures of that dimension, but also alerting those in this realm to the sounds of the Buddha's teachings, waking them, as it were, from their slumber or trance. Their pleasures are temporary, sounds the lute: they are forgetting the sufferings of others; they are resting on their laurels and will one day fall from grace.

Psychologically, difficulties with confluence are of at least two types: a clinging to what comes to be an unhealthy confluence and a pulling back from, or estrangement from, healthy confluence. In the first category are those who demand the sense of at-one-ness from their children, lovers, friends, parents, co-workers, or other intimates and who refuse to allow the necessary "otherness" that permits those others to breathe. These are people who become frightened by the loss of connection, who stifle their own aggressive urges because such urges are "selfish," and who find others' wishes intolerable when they conflict with their own wishes. They are the "enablers" in alcoholic families or the "codependents" in neurotic ones. In the second category are those who, usually because of early deprivations or prodding into independence, crave, and yet are made anxious by, the ego dissolution of confluence. Never having sufficiently experienced the relaxation of the parental embrace in early childhood, they are understandably frightened by the approach of its corollary in adulthood, and they tense, or pull back, at the moment of orgasm, guarding the very ego boundaries that they were induced to create prematurely. They are usually unaware of this tensing and feel cheated somehow, but they cannot recognize the source of their feeling of continued isolation.

A friend of mine named James, for example, remembers a critical moment in his adolescence that baffled and bothered him for the next twenty years. It came as a result of his first taste of the God Realm. At age sixteen, just after having gotten his driver's license, he asked out a young woman on whom

he had silently had a crush for two years. Their blissful evening
culminated in several hours of making out after her parents had
gone to bed, and he felt happier than he could ever remember
feeling. But he went home that night and never called her
again, and he never understood why. This same man, twenty
years later, was made unduly anxious when his wife had a need
to withdraw from him, when her emotional experience did not
match his own. His relationship to the God-like state of confluence was very fragile. As an adolescent, he had both sought
the experience and fled from it; as an adult, he could not bear
to see it dissolve, having no confidence in his own capacity to
re-create it. He was made anxious by both its presence and its
absence.

As an essential component of the Wheel of Life, the God
Realm represents the person's ability to relax ego boundaries,
to dissolve temporarily, to acknowledge the joy of connection
and of aesthetic and intellectual pleasures. It is the place of
reverberation and resonance that the psychoanalyst Michael
Eigen has described as the inexhaustible "nuclear joy kernel"
that causes the infant to smile.[6] Experiences in this realm,
according to the Buddhists, are part of the human capacity and
need not be feared. They are routinely accessed in meditation
practice, for instance, but they are no more sustainable than are
the sensory pleasures that so preoccupied Freud. In fact, when
they become the object of craving, they themselves become a
potent cause of suffering. Freud's powerful descriptions of mystical experiences as "oceanic" fit neatly into this cosmology:
there are indeed meditation experiences that evoke an oceanic
feeling of oneness with the universe, but these are experiences
of the God Realm; they are not the mystical experiences that
the Buddha described as essential to his psychology of analytic
meditation.

THE REALM
OF THE JEALOUS GODS

The Realm of the Jealous Gods (or Titans) is sometimes depicted as a part of the God Realm and sometimes as its own area. In either case, the two sets of beings are separated by a fruit-laden "wishing-tree," over whose fruits the Jealous Gods are fighting. These beings, which embody the ego's aggressive strivings, are trying to garner the fruits of the gods through relentless competitive force. They represent the energy that is needed to overcome a frustration, change a situation, or make contact with a new experience. When the contact is accomplished, it yields the gratification of the God Realm, but it is the Jealous Gods who embody the aggressive force necessary to approach, destroy, and assimilate the obstacles to that satisfaction.

It is interesting that this realm of ego and aggression is presented as one of the upper realms, despite Buddhism's reputation as passive, stoical, and anti-ego. The classic ego functions of taming, mastery, self-control, and adaptation are clearly valued in the Buddhist cosmology. Indeed, they form the basis for the key meditation practice of mindfulness, in which the ego functions themselves are recruited for the cultivation of moment-to-moment awareness. The Bodhisattva of Compassion appears in this locale wielding a flaming sword, symbolic of discriminating awareness. The presence of this sword reinforces the point that the aggressive nature of ego is not seen as the problem; this energy is in fact valued and is necessary in the spiritual path. The objects of this striving, the fruits of the wishing-tree, are seen as ultimately disappointing, however. The Bodhisattva of Compassion urges the Jealous Gods to redirect their aggression, destroying and assimilating the unawareness that keeps them estranged from themselves. In just this way, meditation practice seeks to kidnap the various ego functions, reorienting them away from attempts at possession of "things" and toward the achievement of discriminating awareness. In order to accomplish this, however, the ego functions themselves must first be freed.

This freeing of the ego functions is often the task of psychotherapy. One patient of mine, a writer who was having trouble completing a project that she seemed very excited about, remembers her father always telling her that she was getting "too excited" as she rushed to tell him about her experience, even as she felt that he had no time for her. "If you put a broom up your ass, you could sweep while you go," he would say. So she learned to clamp down on her excitement, keeping everything under control and her body rigid, and developed disabling headaches as a consequence. Her aggressive, excited energy was turned back on her own body rather than enjoyed and used to accomplish something. The idea that she could savor her excitement came as a revelation and a challenge.

A former neighbor of mine showed his estrangement from this important ego function in another characteristic way. He would brood and sulk, rather than directly approach a person from whom he desired something. In his adult life, he manifested this most directly with his lover, with whom he would become petulant and demanding in an unspoken way that attempted to make the lover do his aggressive work for him. Rather than approach his lover when he wanted sex, for instance, he would languish in an aggressively forlorn state while imagining him, the lover, having sex with previous boyfriends. His anger emerged in his dreams, he confided to me, but even then, found no real outlet. In one such dream, for example, after he tried to attack as his lover fled in a spaceship, the scene changed dramatically to reveal an endless, desolate desert where everything was immobile, beautiful, and lonely. His fantasies and dreams defined what he did with this crucial energy of the Jealous Gods: he paralyzed himself, cut himself off from his own aggression, and, like the beings of the Hell Realms, began to experience that aggression as directed against himself by his loved one through the lover's imagined infidelity. He was left bereft, immobile, and out of touch.

THE HUMAN REALM

As a representation of the neurotic mind, then, the Wheel of Life shows not just how beings can be self-indulgent but also how they hide from themselves. The developing infant needs to hate in order to truly love, sexual passion must be lived in order to understand its limitations, fantasies of gratification of unfulfilled needs must be understood as fantasies in order for actual gratification to be appreciated, ego functions must be freed in order to use them for spiritual, as well as worldly, purposes, and ego boundaries must be temporarily relaxed in order for confluence to be understood as a natural outcome of satisfying contact instead of some kind of unapproachable heaven state. It is in the Human Realm that this tendency to hide from oneself is most pronounced, however.

If the lower realms are concerned, as Freud was, with unacceptable *desires*, and if the God Realm and Realm of the Jealous Gods are the province of ego functions and their temporary dissolution, then the Human Realm is concerned with what has come to be known as the self (or the lack thereof). More accurately, it is the realm of the *search* for self, the central concern of the relatively recent psychology of narcissism and in some way the abiding concern of all creative activity. The Bodhisattva of Compassion appears in this domain in the form of the historical Buddha, Sakyamuni, an Indian prince of the fifth century B.C., who is depicted with the alms bowl and staff of an ascetic engaged in the accepted Buddhist strategy of the search for identity.

The central predicament of the Human Realm is that we do not really know who we are. As Winnicott was fond of proposing, "Although healthy persons communicate and enjoy communicating, the other fact is equally true, that *each individual is an isolate, permanently non-communicating, permanently unknown, in fact unfound.*"[7] We are aware of vague and disturbing feelings of emptiness, inauthenticity, and alienation, and we have some sense of the lack of acknowledgment, attention, or recognition—of what the psychoanalysts call mirroring—that might lie behind these disturbing feelings. But we are fundamentally unsure.

We can see how this feeling is passed through the generations. When a child, seeking contact with another person rather than just instinctual gratification, comes up against a narcissistic parent, too preoccupied with her own search to attend to the child's, the child is left with a feeling of absence that becomes the seed of her own fear and insecurity. Such a child is forced to construct what Winnicott called a "False Self" to manage the demands of the alternatively intrusive and ignoring parent. The person then struggles against this necessary construction, the false self, in the attempt to feel real. The false self is created to deal with an impossible situation; as a construction, it eventually rigidifies and obscures more spontaneous personal expressions, cutting the person off from herself. Part of Winnicott's point is that the child of a narcissistic parent has reason to hide from that parent once she has felt that parent's lack of interest. As Winnicott commented, "It is joy to be hidden but disaster not to be found."[8]

A patient of mine, a thirty-year-old painter named Lily, gave me a good description of the genesis of this sense of falseness in the memory of an incident from her childhood. She remembers discovering a paisley shirt in her attic when she was about six years old and insisting on wearing it to school the next day without a jacket so that she could show off her new find. Her mother grew enraged, insisted that she wear a coat, and finally blurted out, "What kind of mother will people think I am? You are a reflection of me!" Lily remembers going to school the next day, with her jacket on, thinking, "*I* am invisible; I am nothing but a reflection of my mother!"

I once saw a patient, another psychotherapist, who began her therapy with the image of herself as a five-year-old girl in pigtails who was hiding behind a huge billboard proclaiming all of her achievements. Her fantasy was of being rescued from behind the billboard. But, mindful of Winnicott's injunctions, I asked her only how it felt to be noticed in such a good hiding place.

From the Buddhist perspective, the Human Realm is not just about the false self but is also about the possibility of transcendent insight into the true nature of self. It is here that the Buddhist concept of *sunyata* (emptiness) can be appreciated. The Buddhists assert that the more we grasp emptiness, the more we feel real—that the core, the incommunicado element, is really a place of fear at our own insubstantiality. This is why we defend it so fiercely, why we do not want to be discovered, and why we feel so vulnerable as we approach our most personal and private feelings of ourselves. In approaching that privacy without fear, the Buddhist practices make possible a sense of genuine liberation rather than permanent isolation.

GREED, HATRED, AND DELUSION

At the core of the Wheel of Life, circling endlessly, are the driving forces of greed, hatred, and delusion, represented by a red cock, a green snake, and a black hog, each one biting the tail of its neighbor, to indicate their interconnectedness. These are the forces that perpetuate our estrangement from ourselves and that keep us bound to the wheel, unable to appreciate the insights of the Buddha and imprisoned by our own runaway minds. Our confusion about ourselves, our fear and insecurity, our ignorance or delusion, in the Buddhist parlance, keep us grasping at pleasant experiences and rejecting of unpleasant ones, despite the fruitlessness of such efforts.

The first wave of psychoanalysis, the classical period of Freud and his followers that extended into the 1950s, was primarily concerned with uncovering repressed desire and anger, or Eros and Thanatos, the life and death instincts, which in some way correspond to the Buddhist mandala's snake and cock. The next wave, of object relations and narcissism that has dominated the past thirty years, exposed the gap within: the emptiness, inauthenticity, or alienation that results from estrangement from our *true selves* and our confusion or ignorance about our own true natures. In the Buddhist view, this is the black hog of delusion, the root or precondition of greed and hatred. Psychoanalysts have been able to identify ignorance, but they have not been able to work with it directly, beyond postulating the incommunicado self that had to be let alone. This was certainly an advance: exposing our narcissism is an essential precondition for transforming it. But the meditative traditions are where we find a lucid methodology for working directly with our confusion about ourselves.

It is tempting to see Buddhism as advocating *escape* from the Wheel of Life and psychotherapy as encouraging *adjustment* to it, and this is in fact what a number of early translators, teachers, and students of Buddhism proposed. Yet, as noted earlier, it is an axiom of Buddhism that nirvana *is* samsara. The Bodhisattva images inset into each realm of the Wheel of Life imply that it is possible to learn *another way* of relating to the emotions of each dimension. This is the sense in which the enlightened person is said to be in the world but not of it.

This vision differs markedly from that held by many in the psychoanalytic community who tend to view the forces of greed, hatred, and delusion as instincts or drives that, by definition, could not develop or mature. Indeed, there is a sharp division within the psychoanalytic field about whether to view the sexual and aggressive drives as capable of development and maturation at all. On the one hand are those who see the id as a "seething cauldron" of primitive energy that must be mastered or regulated and kept under firm control. On the other hand are those who see the possibility of transformation of the infantile drives through the process of giving them "access to consciousness."[9]

The Buddha's vision is definitely of the latter persuasion. The entire Wheel of Life is but a representation of the possibility of transforming suffering by changing the way we relate to it. As the Buddha taught in his final exhortation to his faithful attendant Ananda, it is only through becoming a "lamp unto yourself" that enlightenment can be won.

Liberation from the Wheel of Life does not mean escape, the Buddha implied. It means clear perception of oneself, of the entire range of the human experience: "Things are not what they seem," says the *Lankavatara Sutra*, which was translated into Chinese in 443 A.D. "Nor are they otherwise.... Deeds exist, but no doer can be found."[10]

This emphasis on the lack of a particular, substantive *agent* is the most distinctive aspect of traditional Buddhist psychological thought; it is the realization that transforms the experience of the Wheel of Life. But such a conception is not completely outside the realm of psychoanalysis. True thoughts "require no thinker," the psychoanalyst W. R. Bion echoed. When psychotherapists are identified with their insights, he maintained, their contributions become "psychoanalytically worthless."[11]

It is in this idea of "thoughts without a thinker" that psychoanalysis has approached the Buddhist view, for it is the elimination of narcissism that Bion is suggesting, a possibility that Buddhism also holds dear. The entire thrust of the Buddha's teaching was directed toward trying to convey this as a real possibility. He was at first reluctant even to attempt to communicate his realization, fearing that no one would grasp it. But he ultimately relented, and then formulated his first teachings as the Four Noble Truths: suffering, its cause, its cessation, and the path to its cessation. The Buddha's first truth highlights the inevitability of humiliation in our lives and his second truth speaks of the primal thirst that makes such humiliation inevitable. His third truth promises release and his fourth truth spells out the means of accomplishing that release. In essence, the Buddha was articulating a vision of a psyche freed from narcissism. His Four Noble Truths are the key to understanding the Buddhist psychology of mind.

CHAPTER 2

HUMILIATION: THE BUDDHA'S FIRST TRUTH

The Buddha attained enlightenment in his thirty-fifth year after a six-year struggle with himself. Resting, reflecting, and fasting under the Bodhi tree for seven weeks after his realization, the Buddha appears to have been embarrassed by his discovery. His inclination was to remain silent, to keep his understanding to himself, to assume that no one would take him seriously. He appeared disinclined to teach, and it is said that only after the great god Brahma implored him three times that he finally agreed to expound his teachings.

> This Dhamma which I have realized is indeed profound, difficult to perceive, difficult to comprehend, tranquil, exalted, not within the sphere of logic, subtle, and is to be understood by the wise. . . . If I were to teach this Dhamma, the others would not understand me. That will be wearisome to me, that will be tiresome to me. . . .
>
> With difficulty have I comprehended. There is no need to proclaim it now. This Dhamma is not easily understood by those who are dominated by lust and hatred. The lust-ridden, shrouded in darkness, do not see this Dhamma, which goes against the stream, which is abstruse, profound, difficult to perceive and subtle. . . .
>
> As I reflected thus, my mind turned into inaction and not to the teaching of the Dhamma.[1]

The Buddha ultimately relented, of course, and set out on a forty-five-year period of wandering and teaching. But his initial hesitations bear remembering as we attempt to understand his discoveries in the context of contemporary psychology. The Buddha's teachings are still "against the stream," "difficult to comprehend," and "not within the sphere of logic." They are not what we want to hear. In psychological terms, the Buddha's first truth, for instance, is really about the inevitability of our own humiliation. His insights challenge us to examine ourselves with a candor that we would prefer to avoid.

WHAT THE BUDDHA TAUGHT

When my uncle Howard, an irreligious middle-level IBM executive who loved Bach, his violin, Chinese food, and my aunt, lay dying of leukemia in the Sloan-Kettering Cancer Center several years ago, his thoughts of impending death were tempered somewhat by a sudden realization. Wracked with pain, emaciated and frail, his body breaking down, but still with a faint and rueful smile, he whispered to his wife, "At least I won't have to take another shit." As Beckett would portray it: the human condition.

In his teachings on suffering, the Buddha made clear that some kind of humiliation awaits us all. This is the truth that he felt could be apprehended by those with "little dust in their eyes." No matter what we do, he taught, we cannot sustain the illusion of our self-sufficiency. We are all subject to decay, old age, and death, to disappointment, loss, and disease. We are all engaged in a futile struggle to maintain ourselves in our own image. The crises in our lives inevitably reveal how impossible our attempts to control our destinies really are. At some point, we all find ourselves in the position of my uncle, caught between decay and death.

The Four Noble Truths take this vulnerability as a starting point, cultivating humility out of the seemingly oppressive and inescapable humiliations of life. Far from the pessimistic religion that Buddhism has been portrayed to be, it is, in fact, relentlessly optimistic. All of the insults to our narcissism can be overcome, the Buddha proclaimed, not by escaping from them, but by uprooting the conviction in a "self" that needs protecting. The teachings of the Four Noble Truths describe this possibility explicitly; they are less about religion (in the Western sense) than they are a vision of reality containing a practical blueprint for psychological relief. Positioning our need for a "solid" self squarely in the center of human suffering, Buddhism promises a kind of relief that is beyond the reach of the psychotherapeutic method, brought about through techniques of self-examination and mental training unknown to the West. Happiness is a real possibility, taught the Buddha, if we can but penetrate our own narcissism.

DUKKHA

The Buddha gave his first teachings, preserved in a *Sutra*, or revered collection of sayings, called *Setting in Motion the Wheel of Truth* (*Dhammacakkappavattana Sutta*), in a deer park in a village known today as Sarnath, outside the ancient Indian city of Benares, to an audience of five ascetics with whom he had practiced before his realization. It was as if he was testing his ability to explain his understanding to his old friends and fellow renunciates from whom he had earlier broken. "Now this, Brothers, is the Noble Truth of Suffering!" he proclaimed.

> Birth is suffering, decay is suffering, disease is suffering, death is suffering, sorrow, lamentation, pain, grief and despair are suffering, to be united with the unpleasant is suffering, to be separated from the pleasant is suffering, not to get what one desires is suffering. In brief the five aggregates of attachment (the basis for the human personality) are suffering.[2]

While "suffering" is the conventional translation for the Buddha's word *dukkha*, it does not really do the word justice. A more specific translation would be something on the order of "pervasive unsatisfactoriness." The Buddha is speaking on a number of levels here. Life, he says, is filled with a sense of pervasive unsatisfactoriness, stemming from at least three sources.

First, physical illness and mental anguish are inescapable phenomena in our lives: old age, sickness, and death clash with our wishful fantasies of immortality and therefore contribute to our sense of dissatisfaction. Second, our own likes and dislikes contribute to this sense of dukkha. Not to obtain what one desires causes dissatisfaction, being stuck with what one does not desire causes dissatisfaction, and being separated from what one cherishes causes dissatisfaction. Third, our own personalities contribute to this sense of general unease. As many a psychotherapist can testify, and as the Buddha so clearly recognized, our own selves can feel somehow unsatisfactory to us. We are all touched by a gnawing sense of imperfection, insubstantiality, uncertainty, or unrest, and we all long for a magical resolution of that dis-ease. From the very beginning, the human infant is vulnerable to an unfathomable anxiety that survives in the adult as a sense of futility or as a feeling of unreality. Hovering between two opposing fears—one of isolation and the other of dissolution or merger—we are never certain of where we stand. We search for definition either in independence or in relationship, but the ground always feels as if it is being pulled out from beneath our feet. Our identity is never as fixed as we think it should be.

THE IMAGE OF SELF

The original Greek myth of Narcissus derives its power from just this core uncertainty about the reality of the self. Enamored of his own image, unable to tear himself away from his reflection in a pond, Narcissus died of languor. The power of his image was such that Narcissus gave himself over to it. He was captivated by the completeness of the image, which alleviated his sense of unreality and gave him something (apparently) solid to hang on to. Not only was the reflection illusory, of course, but Narcissus perished by virtue of his attachment to this image of perfection.

Consider again the Buddhist perspective on this captivating image of self, as articulated by the Buddha in that first teaching:

> All worry about the self is vain; the ego is like a mirage, and all the tribulations that touch it will pass away. They will vanish like a nightmare when the sleeper awakes.
>
> He who has awakened is freed from fear; he has become Buddha; he knows the vanity of all his cares, his ambitions, and also of his pains.
>
> It easily happens that a man, when taking a bath, steps upon a wet rope and imagines that it is a snake. Horror will overcome him, and he will shake from fear, anticipating in his mind all the agonies caused by the serpent's venomous bite. What a relief does this man experience when he sees that the rope is no snake. The cause of his fright lies in his error, his

ignorance, his illusion. If the true nature of the rope is recognised, his tranquillity of mind will come back to him; he will feel relieved; he will be joyful and happy.

This is the state of mind of one who has recognised that there is no self, that the cause of all his troubles, cares, and vanities is a mirage, a shadow, a dream.[3]

Far from the narcissistic pursuit that many psychoanalysts and religious scholars have labeled it, Buddhist meditation is rather an attempt to break through and expose narcissism in its every haunt. The Buddha sees us all as Narcissus, gazing at and captivated by our own reflections, languishing in our attempted self-sufficiency, desperately struggling against all that would remind us of our own fleeting and relative natures. His message is a wake-up call. He seeks to rouse us from our Narcissus-like reverie, to redirect our attention from a preoccupation with shoring up an inevitably flawed sense of self to knowledge of what he calls "the Noble Truth."

Birth, old age, sickness, and death are distasteful not just because they are painful but also because they are humiliating. They violate our self-regard and are blows to our narcissism. In one of his first writings about this, Freud recognized that the inability to tolerate unpleasant truths about oneself was essential to narcissism. The Buddha's teachings make this observation the cornerstone of his psychology. We are all subject to this tendency, taught the Buddha. We do not want to admit our lack of substance to ourselves and, instead, strive to project an image of completeness, or self-sufficiency. The paradox is that, to the extent that we succumb to this urge, we are estranged from ourselves and are *not real*. Our narcissism requires that we keep the truth about our selves at bay.

THE VOICE OF THE ANALYST

Psychoanalysis has, of course, come up against this universal sense of inadequacy without any input from the Buddha and has addressed it from several important angles, each of which fleshes out in some important way the Buddhist declaration about dukkha. As each new movement has arisen within the field, the explanations for this universal dissatisfaction have correspondingly shifted so that, overall, there is a trend away from a sexual etiology and toward an emotional one. While first Freud and then Wilhelm Reich explored the genital basis for pervasive unsatisfactoriness, subsequent waves of thought have emphasized restrictions in the capacity for love as a more basic cause of human suffering. Taking these views into account, we might rewrite the Buddha's words as the following: "Birth is suffering, decay is suffering, disease is suffering, death is suffering, the search for ultimate satisfaction through sexuality is suffering, not to be able to love is suffering, not to be loved enough is suffering, not to be known is suffering, to not know oneself is suffering."

Freud traced the universality of human suffering to the co-existence of two irrefutable facts: first, the young child's helplessness and dependence; second, the same child's psychosexual prematurity. Young children have sexual urges that are incompatible with their genital capacities; they desire their parents sexually but are unable to achieve satisfaction with them and so are left with an ongoing sense of inadequacy. Those childhood sexual desires can never be quenched, and many adults cannot settle for mature sexual satisfaction and are compelled instead to search for some kind of unattainable imagined sexual fulfillment that has been wished for since early childhood. As Freud described it:

This early efflorescence of infantile sexual life . . . comes to an end in the most distressing circumstances and to the accompaniment of the most painful feelings. Loss of love and failure leave behind them a permanent injury to self-regard in the form of a narcissistic scar, which in my opinion . . . contributes more than anything else to the "sense of inferiority" which is so common in neurotics.[4]

Therapists constantly see remnants of the condition that Freud articulates. They are in many ways examples of what it is like to be stuck in an Animal Realm on the Wheel of Life. A friend of mine, an accomplished actress named Amy, provides a good illustration. She was previewing in a new play that was probably the most challenging she had yet undertaken. Her parents chose this time to vacation on the West Coast, where her younger sister lived with her husband and year-old child. This was not a new pattern for Amy's parents. They were often not present for the major moments of Amy's career and would manage to miss the entire run of this play, too, since spending time with their grandchild was more important to them. Amy's initial reaction, quite understandably, was to feel scorned and inadequate. Her parents' lack of interest in her work or their inability to appreciate it touched a raw nerve. At base, it resurrected her earlier (and Freud would say "eroticized") desire for their undying admiration, and it threatened to make her unable to receive *any* gratification from her current achievements. It was as if the only feedback that mattered was from her parents.

For Freud, the core narcissistic blow results from an "unbridgeable gap between desire and satisfaction": the adult is never able to gratify his childhood sexual fantasies.[5] In Buddhist terms, this would be a psychodynamic explanation for at least the second of what are traditionally described as the "two sicknesses," namely, the belief in a fixed and abiding self (the *internal sickness*) and the desire for a "real" object (the *external sickness*). No object (or person) could ever feel sufficiently real unless it could actually gratify the original desire for sexual union with the parent. Without such satisfaction, the so-called object is always felt to be wanting, or not real enough.

Reich took the idea of a sexual etiology for dissatisfaction even more concretely than Freud did. Holding open the possibility that completely satisfying sexual relations can occur, Reich made direct sexual gratification the therapeutic goal of his treatments, and he focused on the "muscular armoring," or rigidity, that can detract from satisfying sexual discharge and can make "the rhythm of tension and relaxation impossible."[6] Reich's interest was in how we carry and perpetuate inadequacy in our very bodies. His goal was to open up the character, to make the person less rigid, more "mobile" and spontaneous, more available to emotional, and especially to sexual, experience. In terms of the Wheel of Life, Reich tried to move from the Animal Realm of desire to the God Realm of satisfaction.

As psychoanalytic thought developed, Reich's ideas of muscular armoring were in some way adapted from an emphasis on inhibitions of sexual discharge to more of a focus on inhibitions of the human heart. Otto Rank provided an important, if often overlooked, bridge between the two views. Rank moved the theory from genital orgasm to a kind of ego orgasm, describing how the ego seeks to "unburden itself" through its love relations, freeing itself from inner tensions and inhibitions by "making use" of another person in sex or love. "The ego," said Rank, "is always ready to unravel its ego structure in object relations as soon as it finds objects and situations suitable for its purpose."[7] When the ego is not able to "unravel its structure," when the capacity for love is shut down because of fear, insecurity, or confusion, then the person becomes isolated by and imprisoned in individuality. Where there is no unburdening and no rhythm of tension and relaxation, there can be no freedom to bond, no surrender of ego boundaries, and no merging of the kind that characterizes all forms of love. Without this, the person experiences herself only in isolation, not in connection, and individuality becomes the equivalent of anxiety, rather than one essential and inseparable part of an ever-evolving process of separation and union.

As Rank described it, our basic suffering is rooted in a kind of original separation anxiety, which he called a "fear of life." We fear what has already irrevocably happened—separation from the greater whole—and yet we also come to fear the loss, in death, of this precious individuality. "Between these two fear possibilities," Rank wrote, "these poles of fear, the individual is thrown back and forth all his life, which accounts for the fact that we have not been able to trace fear back to a single root, or to overcome it therapeutically."[8]

What about this fear of individuation and isolation? Is this not the doorway to the insecurities about the self that the Buddha finds so important? Is not Narcissus trying to screen out such fears through his fixation on his own image? Is not the yearning for a fixed and eternal true self designed to counter just such a fear? The problem of inauthenticity, of a restless, insecure, and doubting self, is what has come to dominate psychoanalytic thought in our own time. It is also what has made the Buddha's teachings so relevant, because the Buddha, after his initial hesitation, spoke directly and explicitly to this very problem of identity confusion.

More than any other analyst, D. W. Winnicott explored the terrain of the private self. Conscious, above all, of the fragility of the emerging individual, of her need for silent support in the difficult process of growing up, Winnicott was a master at articulating the ways in which we shut ourselves down, complying with parental demands that stem from parental anxiety rather than the needs of the child. We "impose a coherence on ourselves,"[9] taught Winnicott, if the parental environment is not resilient enough to tolerate our falling apart, to allow our egos to unburden. This *imposed coherence* is what he called "False Self." Analogous to Reich's muscular armoring, Winnicott's false self offers protection against exploitation or lack of interest. "It is a primitive form of self-sufficiency in the absence of nurture,"[10] a strategy of "compliance"[11] that permits the person to survive while hiding out from the unsympathetic parental environment. For Winnicott, and the therapists who have followed in his wake, it was the rigidity of the false self that was responsible for the ongoing sense of dissatisfaction. Prematurely separated from the nourishing attention of the mother, people lose touch with their own bodies and retreat to the confines of their minds; the thinking mind thus becomes the locus of the sense of self. But this is a disappointing and dissociated compromise, an imperfect solution that perpetuates the original deprivation and reinforces the notion of an isolated mind incapable of aliveness or spontaneity. Dukkha, for Winnicott, was the permanent isolation of the individual.

LOST HORIZONS

All of these theories share the idea of an original state of perfection, fantasized or real, toward which the person strives but which is forever unreachable. Whether it be the imagined sexual satisfaction of Freud's genital stage or the earlier experience of effortless mother-infant attunement, the theories all suggest that the person rejects relative pleasures in favor of an unattainable fantasy. "That which he projects ahead of him as his ideal is merely his substitute for the lost narcissism of his childhood," said Freud, "the time when he was his own ideal."[12] Sometimes, when the pattern of such seeking repeats itself enough times, a person will enter psychotherapy.

From a Buddhist perspective, the exploration of the pattern, as would occur in most therapies, is only a start. At root, the person must find a way of confronting, or tolerating, his or her inherent sense of uncertainty. An old friend of mine, a woman named Sara, resisted dealing with her version of this uncertainty for so long that many of her friends thought she could never break her pattern of behavior. For, over a period of close to twenty years, Sara developed a succession of obsessive attachments to supposedly unavailable men, most of whom she found a way to make at least sexually available. She experienced, in the pursuit of these men, an ability to surrender herself that otherwise escaped her in her life. She was able to abandon herself to them in a way that each time seemed absolutely essential to her well-being, as she extracted some kind of powerful energy from them that invigorated her and gave her life meaning. Managing to conquer their resistance and submit to them at the same time, she nevertheless tired of them rather quickly once she got them into bed. She approached each relationship with the feeling that *this one* would be the *ultimate* experience that she had been seeking and missing for her entire life, and she was always disappointed.

Whether Sara was replicating an Oedipal attachment to an unavailable father or trying to rediscover an experience of primary mother-child attunement that had been lacking in her childhood was difficult to know. Yet her behavior was incontrovertible. Not only did she feel incomplete but she had great trouble unburdening her ego in love relationships *except* under the extreme conditions of her pursuit of an unavailable man. To expose her insecurities in a more genuine and ongoing relationship felt too threatening to Sara. She feared humiliation if she revealed herself, and despite the urgings of her friends, she resisted going into therapy. Forever in pursuit of an unobtainable fantasy, Sara was chasing her own tail, circling endlessly like the pig, the snake, and the rooster at the center of the Wheel of Life. Seeking a state of perfection that she imagined but could not remember, Sara had not yet come to terms with her own feelings of incompleteness. She needed not just to explore those feelings but to learn *how* to tolerate what she discovered. Therapy could help her to see the patterns in her behavior, but it was meditation that gave her the tools to accept her predicament.

KNOWING OURSELVES

The Buddhist approach posits a core existential insecurity that is beyond the content of any individual story. While psychoanalysis has traced the path whereby a parent's insecurity can be transmitted to a child, Buddhism stresses the inherent impossibility of figuring out who or what we are, with or without "good enough" mothering. We wish to know ourselves securely, to be sure of who or what we are, but we are frustrated from the beginning by one essential contradiction. Just as modern physics has shown that the observer inevitably distorts that which is observed, so too, we, as experiencing subjects, can never know ourselves satisfactorily as object. We cannot experience ourselves indivisibly but must experience ourselves as either subject or object, as knower or as that which is known.

The maturational separation into subject and object poses a problem that mere fusion, as recurs in love relations, does not adequately resolve. As the professor of religion Richard De Martino explained in the classic collaboration *Zen Buddhism and Psychoanalysis*, "The ego naturally comes to confuse being fulfilled with 'being something.' In its attempt as subject to cope with its task of finding itself, it envisages some object-image of itself."[13] But this is a futile and unsatisfying resolution of the problem; the "object-image" is always lacking, precisely because it can never adequately account for the subject. Just as Freud noted that sexual relations always leave one ever so slightly wanting, so the object-image never does the actual experience complete justice.

The Buddha's method of resolving this dilemma was to encourage "not-knowing." "Keep that 'don't know' mind!" screams the Zen master. Cultivate "the faith to doubt," encourages the contemporary Buddhist author Stephen Batchelor. Or as the seventeenth-century Japanese Zen master Takasui taught:

> You must doubt deeply, again and again, asking yourself *what the subject of hearing could be*. Pay no attention to the various illusory thoughts and ideas that may occur to you. Only doubt more and more deeply, gathering together in yourself all the strength that is in you, without aiming at anything or expecting anything in advance, without intending to be enlightened and without even intending not to intend to be enlightened; *become like a child in your own breast* [italics added].[14]

Now, what does it mean to "become like a child in your own breast"? Is this a return to the mother before the loss of fusion, as so many Western analysts have interpreted the Buddhist message? Is this merely another version of the Narcissus myth—searching for the self within one's breast? Or is there a difference? Takasui is not admonishing the meditator to become like a child at *her mother's* breast, after all. He is proposing something new, something that seems, at first glance, impossible.

According to the Buddhists, doubts about the self are inevitable, and they come with the maturational process. There is a way to explore and even to resolve them, they counsel, by going *into* the doubt, rather than away from it; by purposefully disrupting the existing structures, rather than by indulging them. The First Noble Truth of the Buddha asks us, above all, to accept the uncertainties that we otherwise try to ignore. In so doing, we can then appreciate the rest of the Buddha's psychology.

CHAPTER 3

THIRST: THE BUDDHA'S SECOND TRUTH

A WEALTHY PATIENT confided to me that after having a gourmet meal, he craves a cognac. After the cognac, a cigarette; after the cigarette he will start to think about making love; after making love, perhaps another cigarette. Soon, he begins to crave sleep, preferably without any disturbing dreams. The search for comfort through sense pleasures rarely has an end.

The Second Noble Truth of the Buddha takes its cue from this experience. It is traditionally described as the truth of "the arising of *dukkha*," and its central tenet is that the *cause* of suffering is *craving* or *thirst*. The Buddha describes two types of craving, each of which has a counterpart in psychodynamic thought. The first, the craving for sense pleasures, we can grasp immediately. It is what my wealthy patient at first appears to be describing from his experience. The second, what the Buddha called the craving for *existence and nonexistence*, is what we would today call *narcissistic* craving: the thirst for a fixed image of self, as either something or as nothing. It is the craving for security wherever it can be found: in becoming or in death. Behind my patient's desire for sex, I suspect, lies a yearning for merger with Eros that the Buddha might have called the craving for existence. Behind his desire for a dreamless sleep lies the desire for oblivion, which the Buddha would have recognized as the thirst for nonexistence. The two types of cravings are inextricably linked: sense pleasures are often the vehicle for expression of the deeper yearnings.

THE PLEASURE PRINCIPLE

The thirst for sense pleasures is in many ways the Buddhist equivalent of Freud's *pleasure principle*. In early life, said Freud, the state of rest is first disturbed by the demands of internal needs for food, comfort, warmth, and so on. Whatever was needed was originally provided (by the mother) as if by magic, giving the child a feeling of omnipotence and complete control. This feeling that every need could be immediately satisfied, every sense pleasure immediately obtained, or every unpleasurable sensation immediately avoided is the foundation of both narcissistic craving and the thirst for sense pleasures. It is the first organizing principle of the human psyche, the *pleasure principle*; but its persistence, according to both the Buddha and Freud, can be a source of much emotional turmoil. As Freud described it:

> It was only the non-occurrence of the expected satisfaction, the disappointment experienced, that led to the abandonment of this attempt at satisfaction by means of hallucination. Instead of it, the psychical apparatus had to decide to form a conception of the real circumstances in the external world and to endeavor to make a real alteration in them. A new principle of mental functioning was thus introduced; what was presented in the mind was no longer what was agreeable but what was real, even if it happened to be disagreeable. This setting-up of the *reality principle* proved to be a momentous step.[1]

Pleasurable sensory experiences, which are inherently enjoyable, do not themselves force the establishment of the reality principle. But because they cannot be counted on, the single-minded reliance on pleasure has to be replaced. Similarly, the Buddhist view is not pleasure *denying*: it does not counsel rejection of pleasurable experiences, but only of the attachment to them as sources of ultimate satisfaction. Because of their temporary and unreliable natures, they can never adequately satisfy the craving for certainty that we all feel. The Second Noble Truth encourages us to recognize the frustration inherent in the insatiable pursuit of release or satiety, which most of us seek not just for gratification but also for an offsetting of our insecurity or uncertainty. Sense pleasures take our minds off of our predicament, but in so doing they become addictive, perpetuating the very dissatisfaction they are sought after to alleviate.

Similarly, the Buddha's teachings might be read as an attempt to establish this *reality principle* with regard to the appearing self. Just as we distort the true nature of pleasurable sensory experiences, so we also consistently distort the self-feeling, inflating or deflating it in a perpetual attempt to fix an acceptable image of self in the mind. While psychoanalysis has charted the terrain by which this self-inflation or deflation occurs, Buddhism sees it as the inevitable affliction of the grasping mind.

NO CERTAINTY

The Buddha was concerned with how to escape from just this kind of self-created suffering, with how to avoid the pitfalls of self-inflation or -debasement. It is here that the latter parts of the Second Noble Truth, the thirsts for existence and nonexistence, become relevant. Buddha, we must remember, did not teach a speculative psychology; he taught a practical one designed to liberate practitioners from dissatisfaction. "I do not teach theory," he said, "I analyse."[2] He refused to answer questions that would feed either the tendency to cling to some kind of absolute romanticized ideal or that would enable nihilistic distancing, the two trends that are subsumed under the headings of existence and nonexistence and that become the basis for many powerful religious, psychological, and philosophical dogmas. There were, in fact, fourteen subjects that the Buddha repeatedly refused to discuss, all of them searching for absolute certainty:

1) Whether the world is eternal, or not, or both, or neither.
2) Whether the world is finite (in space), or infinite, or both, or neither.
3) Whether an enlightened being exists after death, or does not, or both, or neither.
4) Whether the soul is identical with the body or different from it.

The Buddha taught that to attempt a definitive answer to these questions would give the wrong idea, that to do so would only feed the tendency to cling to an absolute or to nihilistically reject, neither of which he found useful. He never taught the existence of a true self, nor did he ever support the idea of a chaotic universe in which "nothing matters" and individual actions are of no importance. Rather, he encouraged a consistent doubting of all fixed assumptions about the nature of things. In a teaching that he gave to a skeptical follower named Malunkya-putta, he likened the asking of questions about the ultimate nature of things to a man wounded by an arrow refusing to have the arrow taken out until all of his questions about who the assassin was, where he came from, what he looked like, what kind of bow he was using, and what make of arrow had been shot had been addressed. "That man would die, Malunkyaputta," emphasized the Buddha, "without ever having learnt this."[3]

Applying the same logic to the more intimate psychological questions about the nature of the self, the Buddha was equally resistant to being tied down. When asked point-blank by a wanderer named Vacchagotta whether there was or was not a self, the Buddha remained "therapeutically" silent. He later explained to his attendant Ananda (often the recipient of the Buddha's teachings in the Sutras), that there was no way to answer the man's question without reinforcing some erroneous view of self:

> If I, Ananda, on being asked by the wanderer, Vacchagotta, if there is a Self, should have answered that there is a Self, this, Ananda, would have been a siding-in with those recluses and brahmans who are Eternalists. If I, Ananda, on being asked by the wanderer, Vacchagotta, if there is not a Self, should have answered that there is not a Self, this, Ananda, would have been a siding-in with those recluses and brahmans who are Annihilationists. . . . The wanderer, Vacchagotta, already confused, would have been increasingly confused (and he would have thought): "Was there not formerly a Self for me? There is none now."[4]

GRANDIOSITY AND EMPTINESS

There is something oddly familiar to the Western ear in the Buddha's consistent refusal to endorse one or the other side of a hypothetical duality: neither self nor no-self, neither clinging nor condemning, neither existence nor nonexistence. While no psychological language *as we know it* existed in the Buddha's time—no talk of narcissism, no grandiosity, no abandonment depression or mirroring—there were highly developed philosophical systems that in many cases espoused similar psychological concepts. The Buddha seems to have grasped the psychological dimensions inherent in these systems; he speaks in the language of the Second Noble Truth of the longing for existence or nonexistence in their *psychological* forms, what we in the West would call grandiosity or emptiness and which lead inextricably to a pervasive sense of dissatisfaction. Just as Western psychoanalysts have recognized the falseness of either extreme, so the Buddha and the great Buddhist psychologists who have followed in his wake have counseled a Middle Way that is neither one nor the other.

Just as the philosophers of the Buddha's day could be described as either eternalists (who believed in an immortal heaven, God, or real self) or annihilationists (who believed only in the meaninglessness or futility of life), so the human psyche finds comfort in alternately embracing one or the other of these views. They are, in fact, the two poles of the false self: namely, the grandiose self developed in compliance with the parents' demands and in constant need of admiration, and the empty self, alone and impoverished, alienated and insecure, aware only of the love that was never given. The grandiose self, while fragile and dependent on the admiration of others, believes itself to be omnipotent or self-sufficient and so retreats into aloofness or remoteness, or, when threatened, clings to an idealized other from whom it hopes to retrieve its power. The empty self clings in desperation to that which it feels can assuage its hollowness or retreats to a barren void in which it is unapproachable and which reinforces the belief in its own unworthiness. Neither feels entirely satisfactory, but to the extent that we are governed by the demands of the false self, we can envision no alternative.

If the Buddha had answered that there was a Self, he would have reinforced his questioner's grandiosity, that is, the idealized notions of possessing something lasting, unchanging, and special. If he had answered that there was truthfully no Self, he would have reinforced his questioner's sense of alienation and hollowness, a despairing belief in personal nothingness. When asked the ultimate narcissistic question by another follower—"What is the nature of the self?"—the Buddha responded that there is neither self nor no-self. The question, itself, was flawed, the Buddha implied, for it was being asked from a place that already assumed that the self was an entity. As a psychotherapist with a Buddhist perspective, I constantly have to keep in mind this teaching of the Buddha, however difficult it is to digest. People always come to therapy seeking their "true selves," demanding of the therapist in much the same way as Vacchagotta demanded of the Buddha.

IMPLICATIONS FOR THERAPY

Much of the identity confusion that propels a person into therapy or that arises as a result of therapy can be understood from this perspective. People often bring the sense of falseness about themselves to therapy with the expectation of somehow shedding it. If the therapist and patient rush too quickly to try to fill in the gap that the patient describes, an important opportunity, from the Buddhist perspective, can be lost. In the attempt to give form to the self—as most people influenced by Western therapy think they must do—the chance to work with the Buddha's polarity can be missed. Rather than trying to foster the discovery of a true self, the Buddhist approach is simply to bring the two extremes into focus, thereby releasing the unconscious hold that they exert. This is a guiding principle in much of the therapeutic work that I engage in.

With a patient who is troubled by a consistent sense of doubt or insecurity, for example, I will be much more likely to search for the ways in which they seek refuge in feelings of self-sufficiency and emptiness than I will in trying to fix an identity for them prematurely. This approach derives directly from the Buddha's teaching of the Second Noble Truth, for the manifestations of the false self can always be found in the ways in which a person clings to the worlds of existence and nonexistence. By bringing those attachments into awareness, the opportunity for release is generated. A recent patient of mine, for example, a thirty-five-year-old lawyer named Dorothy, expressed her version of this predicament in an especially vivid, and relatively common, dream:

> I was with somebody's parents. They didn't like me much. I was trying to say something but I couldn't. I just couldn't articulate it, I couldn't find the right words. I opened my mouth but the words wouldn't come. I got more and more frustrated. I just wanted to cry or scream, but I couldn't and turned and left.

The false self is often symbolized in such a manner, as an inability to express what one really means. Dorothy's main task in her childhood, as she remembered it, had been to never show any emotion, never to tell her parents what was bothering her because of their fear of emotionality. She had to be "perfect," so she paralyzed herself. Afraid of becoming "too emotional," she remained unconnected to herself and, in her adult life, to others, as well. In complying with her parents' needs, she had lost touch with her own emotional life, and she was terrified about reestablishing that connection. Plagued with numbing feelings of unreality, she had come perilously close to killing herself in the preceding year. She appeared self-sufficient and aloof to those around her, yet she felt empty and desperate and stated quite openly that she had no idea of who she was. Indeed, this seemed a rather essential element of her identity. In her apparent self-sufficiency and remoteness from any emotionality, Dorothy embodied the grandiose end of the Buddha's spectrum; in her secret desperation, she exemplified the empty pole.

In working with Dorothy's dream, it became clear that, even with my prodding, she could not find the words or emotions to express to her parents: her feelings were not available to her. What was available were the two alternatives she had developed to cope with her parents' demands: she could become the perfectly unemotional automaton or the empty and alienated avoider of human contact. As she became clearer about those two alternatives, Dorothy began to break down her identification with them. This is consistent with the Buddha's teachings: the suffering of the false self derives from attachment to the two extremes of self-sufficiency and emptiness. By bringing awareness to those very attachments, they can be released. Dorothy was left, in fact, with much less of a clear idea of who she was, but she began to feel more alive.

Dorothy's story is far from unique. As children, we were all forced to comply with the selfish demands of parents who needed us to *act* in a certain way to meet their needs. We were all given the sense, at those moments, that who we were was somehow wrong and that we had better compensate in some manner. Like Dorothy, we did our best to give our parents what they needed and adjusted ourselves in one (or both) of two ways—through compensatory self-inflation or compensatory self-negation. In either case, we avoided feeling our loved ones' disregard, but in the process of satisfying them, we became estranged from ourselves. As the therapist Alice Miller has so vividly described it in *The Drama of the Gifted Child*:

It is one of the turning points in therapy when the patient comes to the emotional insight that all the love she has captured with so much effort and self-denial was not meant for her as she really was, that the admiration for her beauty and achievements was aimed at this beauty and these achievements, and not at the child herself. In therapy, this small and lonely child that is hidden behind her achievements wakes up and asks: "What would have happened if I had appeared before you, sad, needy, angry, furious? Where would your love have been then? And I was all these things as well. Does this mean that it was not really me you loved, but only what I pretended to be? The well-behaved, reliable, empathic, understanding, and convenient child, who in fact was never a child at all? What became of my childhood? Have I not been cheated out of it? I can never return to it. I can never make up for it. From the beginning I have been a little adult.[5]

The result of such a scenario is invariably a sense of emptiness or hollowness, a panicked feeling of inauthenticity that breaks through and disrupts the prideful image that developed out of the parents' admiration for the child's accomplishments. The power of the Buddha's psychology is such that it speaks directly to this well-documented aspect of contemporary experience, but it does so without exclusively blaming the parents. For it appears that, though we in the West have just discovered the tendency of the psyche to list from one extreme to the other, the Buddha was articulating it long ago.

MISAPPREHENDING THE SELF

Psychoanalysis has laid virtually all of the blame for this outcome on parental deficiencies, attributing the oscillating feelings of grandiosity and emptiness to the child's mixed success at coping with parents' alternating intrusive and ignoring behavior. The phrase *pathological narcissism* has developed to distinguish the debilitating emptiness and fragile self-esteem of a person such as Dorothy from the *healthy narcissism* of the less obviously disturbed. Yet to the Buddhist teacher, the idea of "healthy narcissism" is something of an oxymoron. *Any* narcissism carries the seeds of this clinging to the two extremes, and all of us experience it to one degree or another. It is the inevitable fallout from the transition from the pleasure principle to the reality principle, because we all retain the desire that our wishes will be gratified without our having to ask, that our needs will be met magically. When this does not happen, we get upset and take the reality personally, feeling it as a rejection or as a threat to our emotional stability. It is in a situation such as this that we retreat to positions of aloofness or emptiness, as protection against the threat of disappointment.

Indeed, the Buddha, in his teachings of the Second Noble Truth, did not reserve the cravings for existence and nonexistence for the pathologically afflicted. Like the craving for sense pleasures, they are presented as universal phenomena. Buddha did not lay the blame for the compelling allure of grandiosity or emptiness on inadequate child rearing; there is no Buddhist prescription for raising an enlightened child free from narcissism. According to Buddhist psychology, narcissism is endemic to the human condition; it is an inevitable, if illusory, outgrowth of the maturational process. Buddhist psychologists see narcissism as essentially self-generated, although they would undoubtedly agree that it could be exacerbated by deficient parenting. It is the tendency of the developing mind to impose a false coherence on itself, to become infatuated with the *image* of self, to grasp for an identity by identifying with something or with nothing, to make the self into something *other* than what it actually is. It is this thirst for certainty, this misapprehension of self, that so confuses the mind. The ego, as subject, wishes to know itself securely but cannot and so is forced to pretend, not just to satisfy the demands of parents but to satisfy itself. In the attempt to preserve this illusion of security, the ego races back and forth between the two extremes of fullness and emptiness, hoping that one or the other will provide the necessary refuge.

TRANSPARENT MIND

Buddhist philosophers and psychologists throughout the ages have recognized just how difficult it can be to prevent the mind from trying to find certainty in either a grandiose image or an empty one. Even when the obvious extremes of the false self have been divested, there is a tendency to replace them with subtler versions of the same impulses. Concepts such as universal mind, absolute reality, true self, cosmic consciousness, or underlying void all have surfaced in various Buddhist schools of thought, only to be relinquished once the subtle tendencies of attachment were recognized. The desire for some kind of *essence* of self was as strong in the Buddha's time as it is in our own. As the psychoanalyst Adam Phillips has pointed out in his *On Kissing, Tickling, and Being Bored*, it is exceedingly difficult to maintain a sense of *absence* without turning that absence into some kind of *presence*.[6] Indeed, the most influential school of thought to develop in Buddhist India, the Madhyamika school, which was developed in the second century A.D. by a prolific scholar named Nagarjuna and which persists in Tibetan Buddhism to this day, recognized just this difficulty. Nagarjuna and the Madhyamika scholars who followed in his wake held that *any* assertion about the self was bound to be distorted because it was in the nature of conceptual consciousness to substantialize that which was trying to be understood. One of my patients, when trying to bend her mind around the possibility that no substantive *agent* works in her being, concluded, "I am a gerund." The mind endeavors to make nouns even out of verbs.

As Buddhism developed and propagated, it became exceedingly difficult to maintain this disciplined a view. The idea of an underlying "Buddha-nature" or of a universal colorless "mind" that permeated and united all beings made the Buddha's teachings seem much more accessible and allowed for notions of self to creep continually back into Buddhist thinking. In fact, the *Lankavatara Sutra*, which achieved prominence after its translation into Chinese in 443 A.D., devoted pages and pages to refuting such popular conceptions of nirvana as vacuity, life force, spirit, vital force, primary substance, supreme bliss, or deliverance. All such notions "conceive Nirvana dualistically," said the Sutra. They only result in "setting the mind to wandering about and becoming confused, as Nirvana is not to be found anywhere."[7]

ABANDONING THE TRUE SELF IDEAL

Psychoanalysis has come a long way in peeling off the layers of false self, exposing the complex dynamics by which we build up identities that constrict us rather than propel us forward. But psychoanalysis is not yet free from the tendencies that so alarmed the Buddhist teachers centuries ago. Just as notions of a universal mind kept creeping back into Buddhism, notions of an underlying true self keep surfacing in psychodynamic theory. "True self" is hard to find, but psychotherapists still consider themselves its custodian.

Although D. W. Winnicott clearly stated that "there is but little point in formulating a True Self idea except for the purpose of trying to understand the False Self,"[8] psychoanalysts in his wake have not been so strict in their views. Consider the following from the neo-Winnicottian analyst Christopher Bollas: "The true self [is that which is able to be spontaneous]. . . . The true self listens to a Beethoven sonata, goes for a walk, reads the sports section of a newspaper, plays basketball, and daydreams about a holiday."[9]

In the Buddhist view, a realized being has realized her own *lack* of true self. She is present by virtue of her absence and can function effectively *and* spontaneously in the world precisely because of her ability to see the self as already broken. It is not necessary to impute a true self to imagine qualities that we associate with emotional maturity. Indeed, it may be the absence of grasping for that essential core that unleashes the flood of affect that makes us feel most real. This is the kind of paradox that both Winnicott and traditional Zen masters thrive on: the true self experience that has come to preoccupy Western analysts is achievable most directly through the appreciation of what the Buddhists would call emptiness of self.

As a relationship with any realized Buddhist teacher will reveal, the actions of a person who has understood *emptiness* bear an uncanny resemblance to what we in the West expect from those who have a highly developed sense of self. From the Buddhist point of view, this becomes possible through an understanding that is not regressive, not a return to the breast or the womb, and not a manifestation of true self. Such an experience, the Buddha taught, clears up a lot of confusion. The illustrious Zen master Hakuin (1685–1768), a practitioner of the "great doubt," described his realization as like the sudden experience of "something similar to the breaking of an ice cover or the collapse of a crystal tower. The joy is so great," he said, "that it has not been seen or heard for forty years."[10]

The crumbling of the false self occurs through awareness of its manifestations, not through the substitution of some underlying "truer" personality. The ability to become aware of self-representations without creating new ones is, psychologically speaking, a great relief. It does not mean that we drop the everyday experience of ourselves as unique and, in some way, ongoing individuals, but it does mean that whenever we find ourselves entering narcissistic territory, we can recognize the terrain without searching immediately for an alternative. The Dalai Lama, schooled even today in the intricate logic of the Madhyamika system, compares one who has understood the true nature of self to the experience of a person wearing sunglasses. The very appearance of the distorted color, he says, lets us know that the color is not true. It is possible, he implies, not to be restricted by the narcissistic polarity of grandiosity and emptiness, even if that is the way we think.

The Buddha's Third Noble Truth makes the same point.

CHAPTER 4

RELEASE: THE BUDDHA'S THIRD TRUTH

AFTER SIX YEARS of struggle, culminating in a night of ceaseless contemplation, the Buddha is said to have realized enlightenment at dawn in the moment when the morning star first appeared in the sky. His Third Noble Truth proclaims that this experience is readily accessible to all who cultivate certain essential qualities of mind. Upon reaching his understanding, he spontaneously exclaimed the following paean of joy, as recorded in the classic Buddhist collection of verse, the *Dhammapada*:

> *I wandered through the rounds of countless births,*
> *Seeking but not finding the builder of this house.*
> *Sorrowful indeed is birth again and again.*
> *Oh, housebuilder! You have now been seen.*
> *You shall build the house no longer.*
> *All your rafters have been broken,*
> *Your ridgepole shattered.*
> *My mind has attained to unconditional freedom.*
> *Achieved is the end of craving.*[1]

The whole of Buddhist psychology is encapsulated in this seemingly simple verse, and yet, the Buddha's message has never been easy to fathom. What is the Buddha alluding to in his verse? What was he seeking, what has he broken, what has been shattered? To what do we owe this unusual expression of naked aggression from a man so renowned for his equanimity?

Wandering through the Wheel of Life, through the round of rebirths, or through his own psychological experience, the Buddha has sought but not found the builder of his body and mind. Where did he come from, he is asking, from where does his feeling of 'I' arise? What is the source of the vaguely romanticized notions of self as a *purposive agent*, as a discrete entity, to which we all unconsciously subscribe? The source or housebuilder, the Buddha exclaims, is *craving*, as he spells out in the Second Noble Truth. "Oh, housebuilder [craving]," he cries, "You have now been seen. You shall build the house no longer." In simply seeing his own craving, he appears to have eviscerated it. Here again is the central Buddhist notion of awareness itself being healing. By bringing his thirst into awareness, the Buddha tells us, he has been freed from its consequences: the sorrow of birth and death.

"All your rafters have been broken," he continues, "Your ridgepole shattered." The Buddha is praising the destructive capacity of wisdom, diamondlike in its strength and precision. These rafters refer explicitly to the core forces of greed and hatred that were portrayed in the center of the Wheel of Life as the snake and the rooster. These forces are broken, he declares; they can no longer support a structure that has been exposed as insubstantial. The ridgepole, too, which supports or gives rise to the rafters, is shattered. Here the reference is to the root cause of the afflictive emotions—ignorance, portrayed in the Wheel of Life as the black hog at the heart of the mandala. Ignorance means misapprehension: in Buddhist parlance, it means imputing a sense of solidity in persons or things that is not necessarily there.

Because of our craving, the Buddha is saying, we want things to be understandable. We reduce, concretize, or substantialize experiences or feelings, which are, in their very nature, fleeting or evanescent. In so doing, we define ourselves by our moods and by our thoughts. We do not just let ourselves be happy or sad, for instance; we must become a happy person or a sad one. This is the chronic tendency of the ignorant or deluded mind, to make "things" out of that which is no thing. Seeing craving shatters this predisposition; it becomes preposterous to try to see substance where there is none. The materials out of which we construct our identities become useless and broken when the ridgepole of ignorance is shattered. The Buddha reported that his mind spontaneously attained "unconditional freedom" when he saw his craving clearly, unconditioned by the forces of greed, hatred, or ignorance and therefore free.

SUBLIMATION

It is this unconditional freedom that the Buddha promises in his declaration of the Third Noble Truth. The end of suffering is achievable, he suggests, not through the kind of unconditional love that many Westerners have imagined could alleviate their felt sense of unsatisfactoriness, not through the recapturing of some imagined perfection, but through the unconditional freedom of the enlightened mind: "What, now, is the Noble Truth of the Extinction of Suffering?" asked the Buddha. "It is the complete fading away and extinction of this craving, its forsaking and abandonment, liberation and detachment from it."[2]

The Buddha is suggesting something very radical here: that it is possible to isolate the forces of craving in one's own mind and become both liberated from them and unattached to them merely from seeing that craving for what it is. The contrast with Western psychoanalysis seems at first glance to be particularly stark. One of the fundamental concepts in psychoanalytic theory, after all, is that instinctual drives or forces (erotic, aggressive, or narcissistic strivings) are inborn, inherent, and inescapable. In the psychoanalytic view, we must reconcile ourselves to this fact. The closest that psychoanalysts have come to addressing the kind of mental transformation described in Buddhism is found in their discussions of *sublimation*, in which, as Freud proposed, "the energy of the infantile wishful impulses is not cut off but remains ready for use—the unserviceable aim of the various impulses being replaced by one that is higher, and perhaps no longer sexual."[3] Sublimation, for Freud, held out the possibility of escape from the impossible demands of the "infantile wishful impulses." Is the escape that the Buddha described the same or different?

Listen, for instance, to Freud's description of Leonardo da Vinci's presumed mental state. Were we not to know the identity of the author, we would probably assume him to be a devotee of Eastern mysticism rather than Western science:

> His affects were controlled . . . ; he did not love and hate, but asked himself about the origin and significance of what he was to love or hate. Thus he was bound at first to appear indifferent to good and evil, beauty and ugliness. . . . In reality Leonardo was not devoid of passion. . . . He had merely converted his passion into a thirst for knowledge. . . . When, at the climax of a discovery, he could survey a large portion of the whole nexus, he was overcome by emotion, and in ecstatic language praised the splendour of the part of creation that he had studied, or—in religious phraseology—the greatness of his Creator.[4]

All of the qualities usually attributed to the Buddha are present in Freud's description of the sublimated state of da Vinci: the control of the affects, the transformation of love and hate into intellectual interest, the primacy of investigation, even the climactic ode to the greatness of his Creator. Only in the Buddha's case, the Creator, or housebuilder, is defeated, not extolled.

The vision of the Buddha is that the neurotic aspects of mind—as personified by the pig, the snake, and the rooster of ignorance, hatred, and greed—are *not* essential to the mental continuum. They may be inborn or even instinctual, but they are not intrinsic to the nature of mind. They can be eliminated, or, in psychoanalytic parlance, sublimated to the point of cessation. Most of Buddhist psychology, in fact, is concerned with demonstrating how the narcissistic impulses to identify with or distance oneself from experience can be transformed into wisdom about the true nature of self. This is sublimation of an order that Freud did not often consider, and as we shall see, it is brought about not only through analysis but also through methods of mental training explicitly taught by the Buddha.

ALREADY BROKEN

This point was driven home for me for the first time when I was traveling in Asia in 1978 on a trip to a forest monastery in northeastern Thailand, Wat Ba Pong, on the Thai-Lao border. I was taken there by my meditation teacher, Jack Kornfield, who was escorting a group of us to meet the monk under whom he had studied at that forest hermitage. This man, Achaan Chaa, described himself as a "simple forest monk," and he ran a hundred-acre forest monastery that was simple and old-fashioned, with one notable exception. Unlike most contemporary Buddhist monasteries in Thailand, where the practice of meditation as the Buddha had taught had all but died out, Achaan Chaa's demanded intensive meditation practice and a slow, deliberate, mindful attention to the mundane details of everyday life. He had developed a reputation as a meditation master of the first order. My own first impressions of this serene environment were redolent of the newly extinguished Vietnam War, scenes of which were imprinted in my memory from years of media attention. The whole place looked extraordinarily fragile to me.

On my first day, I was awakened before dawn to accompany the monks on their early morning alms rounds through the countryside. Clad in saffron robes, clutching black begging bowls, they wove single file through the green and brown rice paddies, mist rising, birds singing, as women and children knelt with heads bowed along the paths and held out offerings of sticky rice or fruits. The houses along the way were wooden structures, often perched on stilts, with thatched roofs. Despite the children running back and forth laughing at the odd collection of Westerners trailing the monks, the whole early morning seemed caught in a hush.

After breakfasting on the collected food, we were ushered into an audience with Achaan Chaa. A severe-looking man with a kindly twinkle in his eyes, he sat patiently waiting for us to articulate the question that had brought us to him from such a distance. Finally, we made an attempt: "What are you really talking about? What do you mean by 'eradicating craving'?" Achaan Chaa looked down and smiled faintly. He picked up the glass of drinking water to his left. Holding it up to us, he spoke in the chirpy Lao dialect that was his native tongue: "You see this goblet? For me, this glass is already broken. I enjoy it; I drink out of it. It holds my water admirably, sometimes even reflecting the sun in beautiful patterns. If I should tap it, it has a lovely ring to it. But when I put this glass on a shelf and the wind knocks it over or my elbow brushes it off the table and it falls to the ground and shatters, I say, 'Of course.' But when I understand that this glass is already broken, every moment with it is precious."[5] Achaan Chaa was not just talking about the glass, of course, nor was he speaking merely of the phenomenal world, the forest monastery, the body, or the inevitability of death. He was also speaking to each of us about the self. This self that you take to be so real, he was saying, is already broken.

A SHRUNKEN RESIDUE

Psychoanalysis is quite clear about why this vision of Achaan Chaa's is so difficult to accept: we do not wish to see the glass as already broken. Our life energy, or *libido*, has as its original source the unencumbered union of infant and mother, which the psychoanalysts called primary narcissism. According to Freud, the ego originally includes everything, taking the entire mother-infant conglomeration as its own. Only later does the ego spin off an external world from itself, reducing itself to a "shrunken residue"[6] of the much more pervasive whole that it once encompassed. Yet the state of paradise that predated the emergence of self-conscious desire continues to color our perceptions of the way things are. Its influence does not disappear.

The original feeling of unity persists in the psyche as a driving force toward which the person aspires in adult life. Both in love relations and in our subjective sense of ourselves we attempt to re-create or recapture that original feeling of infantile perfection from which we have all been inexorably divorced. In psychoanalytic terms, the original energy of the mother-child union, the foundation of the pleasure principle, is thought to bifurcate as the child develops. On the one hand is what is called ego libido, in which the self becomes the receptacle of the child's hopes and dreams. On the other hand is what is called object libido, in which other people are felt to contain the key to happiness and so are pursued with the expectation of a kind of re-union. This split between the subjective self yearning for completion and the objective self as a self-sufficient entity heralds the onset of confusion.

From an analytic perspective, all sublimation is really an attempt to transform these energies of ego libido and object libido into a "higher state or plane of existence" where "something of . . . the original unity is in the process of being restored."[7] Eerily echoing the Buddhist philosophers of medieval India, the analytic view contends that sublimation actually urges the individual toward reconciliation of the endless search for perfection. We are all haunted by the lost perfection of the ego that contained everything, and we measure ourselves and our lovers against this standard. We search for a replica in external satisfactions, in food, comfort, sex, or success, but gradually learn, through the process of sublimation, that the best approximation of that lost feeling comes from creative acts that evoke states of being in which self-consciousness is temporarily relinquished. These are the states in which the artist, writer, scientist, or musician, like Freud's da Vinci, dissolves into the act of creation.

PERFECTION OF WISDOM

Using this vocabulary, we can understand the Buddha's truth of cessation in a new way. For, in Buddhism as well as in psychoanalysis, there are also said to be two essential currents of the life energy: wisdom and compassion. These are the two qualities of the enlightened mind, the two forces that are cultivated through meditation and that are spontaneously unleashed with the realization of enlightenment. In the mystical Tantric practices preserved in the Buddhist schools of Tibet, the two primary energy currents of the psychic nervous system that are united in advanced meditative attainments are always explicitly identified with the forces of wisdom and compassion. Psychoanalysis describes these two currents in their infantile states, as ego and object libido, while Buddhism praises them in their sublimated states, as wisdom and compassion. Wisdom is, after all, sublimated ego libido; it is investment in the self turned inside out, the transformation of narcissism and the eradication of ignorance about the nature of self. What kind of conceit is possible, after all, when the self, as in Achaan Chaa's vision, is understood as already broken? Compassion, it follows, is sublimated object libido: desire and rage transformed through the vision of there being no separate subject in need of a magical reunion with either a gratifying or a frustrating Other.

The Buddha's realization of nirvana was actually a discovery of that which had been present all the time. The Buddha did not enter some new territory: he saw things the way they were. What was extinguished was only the *false view* of self. What had always been illusory was understood as such. Nothing was changed but the perspective of the observer. When asked, "What are you?" by an awestruck would-be follower, the Buddha responded only, "I am awake." As one important Mahayana Sutra put it, "If we are not hampered by our confused subjectivity, this our worldly life is an activity of Nirvana itself."[8]

THE WISH

The key concepts of Buddhist psychology—craving, ignorance, and *anatta* (no-soul or no-self)—are all intimately involved with the Buddha's Third Noble Truth. These are the most difficult concepts in all of Buddhism because they attempt to speak to the heart of our misconceptions about ourselves. Fundamentally, the Buddhist teachings assert, we are all still subject to what today's psychologists would call a kind of primary process thinking, a primitive tendency to believe things are the way we wish them to be without regard for reality, logic, or even our own sensory feedback. What is craving, after all, but a wish—a wish for satisfaction, gratification, holding, security, or solidity; a wish for the return of infantile perfection?

Young children reveal this primitive mode of thought most clearly. They see their parents as invulnerable, as icons, immortal and unchanging; they see their parents' relationship in much the same way. We, properly, try to accommodate them in this way of thinking. Nothing is more damaging than for a child to be made prematurely aware of his parents' vulnerability. Yet the outcome of this way of thinking is that the developing child continues to ascribe notions of solidity to both significant others and to himself. There seems to be no good alternative to this developmentally, for if this sense of solidity is not imputed, the child becomes depressed or otherwise emotionally disturbed. When this sense of solidity *is* internalized, however, it survives through a kind of persistence of primary process thinking, in which we repeatedly and unconsciously ascribe attributes of mass to *processes* that are not "things in themselves."[9]

I remember moving to New York and walking up and down

the Manhattan streets and suddenly realizing that none of the ground I was walking on was solid. All of the sidewalks had layers of tunnels running beneath them. "Where was the ground?" I wondered. "Was the whole thing going to collapse?" I suffered a similar disappointment in my childhood when I first realized that turning up the thermostat in my living room did not directly make the room warmer. There was something called a boiler in the basement that had to be invoked and that I did not understand. In my own way, I was unconsciously assuming the solidity of things, wanting them to be the way I imagined.

Freud was responsible for uncovering the primacy of the wish in our unconscious life. As he demonstrated, one of the most common places for this kind of thinking to emerge is in our intimate or erotic relationships. The long-buried attachment to a lost state of perfection is often suddenly exposed in our love relationships, especially when it is first disappointed. We see this often in therapy, where such disappointments can be used as a unique opportunity to confront our expectations for perfection. A friend of mine from medical school, a doctor named Dave, had just this experience when he first fell in love, and he needed quite a bit of therapy to deal with the consequences. In the beginning of his relationship, Dave was filled with a pervasive sense of wonder. Both he and his future spouse felt sure that they had found their true loves, and they married quickly. After a blissful several years together, with deeply satisfying sexual relations, they wanted to have a child. For Dave, his wife embodied perfection. He adored her, loved being in her presence, and especially looked forward to their sexual unions, at which times he felt united with what the psychoanalysts would call his ego ideal, the reflection of his own memory of perfection. As one psychoanalyst puts it in describing such situations, Dave felt "the radiance" of his wife's love falling on, absorbing, and devouring his ego[10] when they had sex. Dave put it somewhat differently in describing it to me, but the meaning was similar.

When his wife became pregnant, however, her sexual desires decreased noticeably, and Dave was devastated and furious. No longer perfect, she became now purely a source of frustration for him. When she could no longer represent the ideal to Dave, she ceased to be of interest to him. He took her sexual lack of interest personally, and, deprived of his access to the blissful state of union that he craved, he could not maintain any sense of connection to his newly pregnant (and nauseated) spouse. Dave's work in therapy involved separating out the image of perfection from the actual person he had married. What he had the most difficulty coming to terms with was how anxious and empty he felt whenever his wife's "imperfections" manifested. He needed to have that perfection, he felt, or his life would have no meaning.

Dave's need was not an unusual one; what was unusual, perhaps, was how close he had come to satisfying it. The anxiety that he became aware of has been recognized as central to the human predicament by Buddhist teachers for centuries. It is only when one's ideal is recognized as a fantasy that this anxiety can be alleviated. As the third Zen patriarch, Seng-tsan, a great Chinese teacher, put it in his *Verses on the Faith Mind*, the greatest source of human anxiety is the experience of nonperfection. Only through the recognition of perfection as a fantasy can such insecurity be overcome; only then can one live "without anxiety about non-perfection."[11]

The wish for security or perfection, for a return to the preanxious state, is one of the most compelling unconscious wishes that we harbor. It is this wish that, in the Buddhist view, drives us to see self and other as fixed, immobile, and permanent *objects* that can be possessed or controlled and that in some way contain a piece of that original security. If the core of our being, as Freud said, consists of these unconscious wishful impulses, imagine the consequences of identifying this so-called core as such. Such a core can simply evaporate.

IGNORANCE

The original satisfaction of primary narcissism, said Freud, is established in the psyche as a memory, which then becomes a model or schema, preserved as an "idea," for what is sought in later life. As Freud described it, the memory of this satisfaction becomes established in the mind as a concrete "thing," which the person either identifies with or tries to re-create. This concretization of experience, which the thinking mind is so expert at carrying out, is what the Buddhists call ignorance. While its consequences emerge in our love relations, it is just as insidious in our misapprehension of ourselves. We expect a certain kind of solidity of ourselves: we impute it, in fact, basing our expectations on the kind of ego feeling that we once experienced at the breast and that we later concretized as a lost perfection.

For the self, according to the Buddha's language of the ancient Sutras, is a fiction—a mirage, a shadow, or a dream. In today's psychodynamic language, we would call it a fantasy, a pretense, or a wish. "The mind," echoed the sixth Zen patriarch, Hui-neng, in the seventh century A.D., "is at bottom an imagination." And, "since imagination is the same as illusion," he concluded, "there is nothing to be attached to."[12] The essential task of meditation is to uncover the unconscious wishful conceptions of self, the fundamental cravings, and to expose them as fantasy, thereby dispelling ignorance and revealing the imagined nature of self. The Third Noble Truth asserts that this is a real possibility. We must turn to the Fourth Noble Truth to find out how to make this realization our own.

CHAPTER 5

NOWHERE STANDING: THE BUDDHA'S FOURTH TRUTH

T HERE IS A famous story in the Zen tradition of China, recounted in the Sutra of the Sixth Patriarch, that illustrates the critical importance of clear thinking when one practices meditation. It is as relevant in today's climate as it was thirteen hundred years ago, for misconceptions about meditation continue to bedevil today's practitioners. A good way of introducing the Buddha's Fourth Noble Truth, this story emphasizes how essential a correct conceptual view can be when one follows the Buddha's example and tries to deal with one's own emotional life.

RIGHT VIEW

Forever alert to the tendency of the human psyche to substitute some kind of imagined state of perfection for true understanding, Hung-jen, the departing fifth patriarch, challenged his students and followers of the seventh century A.D. to compose a verse demonstrating their understanding of the Buddha's teachings. The most satisfactory verse would indicate his

successor. The foremost disciple, Shen-hsiu, who was expected
to assume the role of the master, presented the following:

> *The body is the Bodhi tree,*
> *The mind is like a clear mirror standing.*
> *Take care to wipe it all the time,*
> *Allow no grain of dust to cling.*

A perfectly acceptable response, Shen-hsiu's verse made a virtue
of the empty and reflecting mind, a recurrent motif in Buddhist literature. But the clear mirror, like the true self, too easily becomes an object of veneration. Such a view merely
replaces the concrete self with a more rarefied version that is
then thought to be even more real than the original.

   An illiterate kitchen boy, Hui-neng, grasped the imperfection of Shen-hsiu's response and presented the following alternative:

> *The Bodhi is not a tree,*
> *The clear mirror is nowhere standing.*
> *Fundamentally not one thing exists;*
> *Where then is a grain of dust to cling?*[1]

Hui-neng's response, which was consistent with the teachings
of Nagarjuna and the Madhyamika school in embracing neither absolutism nor nihilism, avoided the trap of idealization
that Shen-hsiu's poem retained. Hui-neng avoided the common misconception of liberation as a mind emptied of its contents or a body emptied of its emotions. The mind, or self,
that we conceive of does not exist in the way we imagine, said
Hui-neng; if all things are empty, to what can we cling? If the
mind itself is already empty, why should it have to be

cleansed? If the emotions are empty, why do they have to be eliminated?

Even in a Buddhist community, this view challenged conventional thinking. The departing fifth patriarch, for example, found it necessary to praise Shen-hsiu's answer in public, while privately rebuking him. Publicly denouncing Hui-neng, the patriarch secretly named Hui-neng the sixth patriarch and then urged him to flee under the cover of darkness. Yet, Hui-neng, in his own way, was articulating what has always been one of the major components of the Buddha's teaching, what has become known as *Right View*.

THE MIDDLE PATH

The Fourth Noble Truth the Buddha articulated in his first teaching at Sarnath was that of the Way leading to the Cessation of Dukkha. Known as the *Middle Path*, it was said to avoid the two extremes of self-indulgence and self-mortification, or, in more contemporary terms, of idealization and denial. Having tried both sets of practices, the Buddha realized that each subtly reinforced the very notions of "I" or "mine" that created the felt sense of suffering in the first place. The search for happiness through sense pleasures he called "low, common, unprofitable and the way of ordinary people," and the search for happiness through denial or asceticism he called "painful, unworthy and unprofitable."[2] Relaxing the ego boundaries and dissolving the sense of self in pleasurable or even ecstatic experiences did not relieve suffering, nor did giving free reign to the emotions. Attacking the body and subjugating the self, coercing the ego into some kind of surrender, also did not relieve suffering, nor did trying to deny the emotions.

The correct approach, taught the Buddha, lay in the ground between these two extremes. It required the alignment of eight specific factors of mind and behavior: understanding, thought, speech, action, livelihood, effort, mindfulness, and concentration. When these factors were properly established, taught the Buddha, they constituted the Path to Cessation. The Eight factors are collectively known as the *Eightfold Path*: the behavioral categories of Right Speech, Right Action, and Right Livelihood are the ethical foundation; the meditative categories of Right Concentration and Right Mindfulness are the foundation of mental discipline traditionally associated with the formal practice of meditation; and the wisdom categories of Right Understanding and Right Thought represent the conceptual foundation that has also been termed Right View. It is this latter category that is often given short shrift by those eager to embark on the meditative path, who then, at best, give answers like Shen-hsiu's.

Consistent with the Buddhist method of approaching an authentic view of self by first bringing the manifestations of false self into awareness, the most effective way of developing the Right View that the Buddha encouraged is to examine the various common manifestations of False View. In doing this, we can see how much our confusion about the nature of our emotions colors our understanding of key words like *ego* or *self*. We do not know what to make of our emotions, and we let our various attempts at dealing with them define our understanding of the Buddha's teaching. To truly follow the Eightfold Path, we must reverse this process. Instead of letting our misconceptions about our feelings influence our understanding, we must let our understanding change the way we experience our emotions.

THE PRIMAL SCREAM

I often have the experience as a therapist of helping someone discover a difficult feeling like anger and then hearing them ask, "What do I do now? Should I go home and have it out?" Sometimes we feel that the only solution is to act out every emotion that we get in touch with. We feel as if we must *express* it to whomever it is directed or that we are somehow cheating ourselves. The idea of simply *knowing* the feeling does not occur to us. This view that emotions will pollute us if we do not get them out is a strongly rooted one that has definite implications for the way in which the Buddha's teachings on selflessness are often misunderstood.

Many meditators, for example, are puzzled by these teachings and mistakenly strive to rid themselves of what they understand to be their Freudian-based egos. Conventional notions of ego—as that which modulates sexual and aggressive strivings—have led many Americans to mistakenly equate selflessness with a kind of "primal scream" in which people are liberated from all constraints of thought, logic, or rationality and can indulge, or act out, their emotions thoroughly. Selflessness is confused here with Wilhelm Reich's organismic potency, and the ego is identified as anything that tenses the body, obscures the capacity for pleasurable discharge, or gets in the way of expressing emotion. Popularized in the sixties, this view remains deeply embedded in the popular imagination. It sees the route to enlightenment as a process of unlearning, of casting off the shackles of civilization and returning to a childlike forthrightness. It also tends to romanticize regression, psychosis, and any uninhibited expression of emotion.

Such a view in fact represents a return to the primary process, from which, as we have seen, the fantasized self is fabricated. By casting off the mental activity and thinking characteristic of the Freudian ego (the so-called secondary process), people with this misconception abandon the ego skills necessary for successful meditation, which is essentially an exercise of ego functions: consciously disciplining the mind and body is nothing if not the task of the Freudian ego. Thus, meditation is not a means of forgetting the ego; it is a method of using ego to observe and tame its own manifestations. Development of the capacity to attend to the moment-to-moment nature of mind allows the self to be experienced without the distortions of idealization or wishful fantasy. Rather than encouraging a consolidated self sure of its own solidity, the Buddhist approach envisions a fluid ability to integrate potentially destabilizing experiences of insubstantiality and impermanence.

This is an important distinction to make in differentiating the Buddhist view from the conventional Western one. We in the West often imagine that the developed self must be the way we see a champion boxer: strong, muscular, confident, and intimidating. The Buddhist view challenges this conception the way the young Muhammad Ali challenged the boxers of his time. For the Buddha, the correct view is consistent with Ali's analogy of "float like a butterfly and sting like a bee": it is a different kind of strength, but it is strength, nonetheless. Attempting to jettison the Freudian ego only undercuts the ego strength that is necessary for successful meditation practice.

UNION

Another popular misconception is that selflessness is some kind of oneness or merger—a forgetting of the self while one simultaneously identifies with the surroundings, a trance state, or an ecstatic union. According to this view, yearning separates one from the ultimate object of one's passion; and if one gives up one's emotions, some kind of ultimate satisfaction can be obtained. This view of selflessness as union has strong roots (it is the one that has been influenced by psychedelic drug use, for example), and it is the traditional psychodynamic explanation, dating from Freud's view of the oceanic feeling. Thus, selflessness is identified with the infantile state before development of the ego: the infant at the breast merged in a symbiotic and undifferentiated union, with no need for any troubling emotion.

The effort in this misunderstanding is to make any difficult emotion disappear. We imagine that we can either replace it with its opposite or induce a numbed state in which nothing need be felt. In union lies the supposed annihilation of the emotions; they can be shed as the individual merges into the state of oneness. People who deal with their anger by always being sweet are using this defense, as are those who seek oblivion in drugs or alcohol. One of the most critical therapeutic tasks for people in recovery from drug or alcohol abuse is to help them find a way to be with their anxieties without rushing to drown those out. The emotionless escape they seek is a vacuity that is the psychic equivalent of the Buddha's longing for nonexistence.

There are, in fact, states accessible in meditation that induce feelings of harmony, merger, and loss of ego boundaries, but these are not the states that define the notion of selflessness. Also, when certain meditation techniques of one-pointedness are pursued with some perseverance, they lead inevitably to feelings of relaxation and tranquility that are soothing and seductive, in which the more troubling emotions are in abeyance. Yet Buddhism always stresses that such states are not the answer to the problem of the emotions. The distinctive attentional strategy of Buddhism is not one-pointedness but mindfulness, or *bare attention*, in which moment-to-moment awareness of changing objects of perception is cultivated. It is this practice that focuses attention on the self-concept and that teaches a different way for one to experience feelings.

But psychoanalytic interpreters, and the naive meditators who have followed in their wake, have drawn inspiration only from the concentration practices, and not from the more essential practices of the so-called Great Doubt. They have emphasized the oceanic experience, but not the more terrifying lack of inherent identity. Physicians who have popularized meditation as a technique of stress reduction have also painted a picture of meditation based solely on accounts of concentration practices, and generations of newly practicing meditators have aspired to dissolve their tensions—and their minds—into the pool of blissful feelings that would make them "at one" with the universe, or the Void. Yet selflessness is not a return to the feelings of infancy, an experience of undifferentiated bliss, or a merger with the Mother—even though many people may seek such an experience when they begin to meditate, and even though some may actually find a version of it. Selflessness does not require people to annihilate their emotions, only to learn to experience them in a new way.

SUBJUGATION

Besides feeling that emotions must be either expressed or repressed, we sometimes imagine a third alternative: that they must be controlled, managed, or suppressed. In this view, the emotions are personified as wild animals lurking in the jungles of the unconscious—animals that must be guarded against or tamed to the greatest extent possible. A friend of mine remembers learning to swim and being afraid of jumping into the deep end of the pool, out of fear that he would be dragged down by the forces hiding there. Only later in life was he able to understand that his fear had been of his own powerful emotions. This fear is the source of the misunderstanding of selflessness as subjugation. With this view, too, the emotions are never understood as empty in their own right. They are perceived as real entities over which the person can have only limited control and which must be managed vigilantly to avert catastrophe.

Because of this view, the self is thought of as something that must be subjugated to a higher power. This notion very quickly enters the territory of thinly disguised masochism, for the tendency is to seek a greater Being to whom one can surrender, subduing one's own emotions in an idealized merger experience where the ego boundaries are temporarily interrupted. The problem here is that the reality of the other is accepted and even revered, while that of the self is denied.

The psychoanalyst Annie Reich, in a classic paper on self-esteem in women, describes this very well. "Femininity," she says, is often "equated with complete annihilation."[3] The only way to recover needed self-esteem is to merge or fuse with a glorified or idealized other, whose greatness or power she can then incorporate. For both sexes, something similar can seem the only option in spiritual circles: the need to see some *one* as embodying the idealized qualities of the awakened compassionate mind can be very strong. The wish, in this case, is (again) for some object, person, or place to concretely represent the sought-after qualities of mind. Meditators with this misunderstanding are vulnerable to a kind of eroticized attachment to teachers, gurus, or other intimates toward whom they direct their desire to be released into abandon. More often than not, they also remain masochistically entwined with these figures to whom they are trying to surrender.

DISAVOWAL

A fourth common misconception, popular in what has become known as transpersonal psychology, is the belief that egolessness is a developmental stage *beyond* the ego—that the ego must first exist and then be abandoned. This is the flip side of the belief that egolessness precedes the development of the ego; instead, egolessness supposedly succeeds the ego. The coping strategy that best defines this misunderstanding is one of disavowal, where troubling emotions are pushed aside or disowned as if they are no longer relevant. They are treated as if they were just a stage that the person had to go through.

This approach implies that the ego, while important developmentally, can in some sense be transcended or left behind. Here we run into an unfortunate mix of vocabulary. Yet listen to the Dalai Lama on this point: "Selflessness is not a case of something that existed in the past becoming nonexistent. Rather, this sort of "self" is something that never did exist. What is needed is to identify as nonexistent something that always was nonexistent."[4] It is not ego, in the Freudian sense, that is the actual target of the Buddhist insight, it is, rather, the self-concept, the *representational* component of the ego, the *actual* internal experience of one's self that is targeted.

The point is that the entire ego is *not* transcended; the self-representation is revealed as lacking concrete existence. It is not the case of something real being eliminated, but of the essential groundlessness being realized for what it has always been. Meditators who have trouble grasping this difficult point often feel under pressure to disavow critical aspects of their being that are identified with the unwholesome "ego."

Most commonly, sexuality, aggression, critical thinking, or even the active use of the first person pronoun *I* are relinquished, the general idea being that to give these things up or let these things go is to achieve egolessness. Meditators set up aspects of the self as the enemy and then attempt to distance themselves from them. The problem is that the qualities that are identified as unwholesome are actually empowered by the attempts to repudiate them. It is not unusual to find meditators insisting in therapy that they do not need sex or had no need for an orgasm, or to find them denying that a frustration was evoking anger. Rather than adopting an attitude of nonjudgmental awareness, these meditators are so concerned with letting *it* (their unwholesome feelings) go that they never have the experience of the insubstantiality of their own feelings. They remain identified with them through the action of disavowal.

In a similar way, those with this misunderstanding of self-lessness tend to overvalue the idea of the "empty mind" free of thoughts. In this case, thought itself is identified with ego, and such persons seem to be cultivating a kind of intellectual vacuity in which the absence of critical thought is seen as an ultimate achievement. As the Buddhist scholar Robert Thurman has written of this misconception: "One just refutes all views, dismisses the meaningfulness of language, and presumes that as long as one remains devoid of any conviction, holding no views, knowing nothing, and achieving the forgetting of all learning, then one is solidly in the central way, in the 'silence of the sages.'"[5]

Contrary to this way of thinking, conceptual thought does not disappear as a result of meditative insight. Only the belief in the ego's solidity is lost. Yet this insight does not come easily. It is far more tempting—and easier—to use meditation to withdraw from our confusion about ourselves, to dwell in the tranquil stabilization that meditation offers, and to think of this as approximating the teaching of egolessness. But this is not what the Buddha meant by Right View.

EMPTINESS

To counter such tendencies, Nagarjuna, the founder of the Madhyamika school of Buddhism, taught the doctrine of emptiness, or *sunyata*. Emptiness, he understood, is not a thing in itself, but is always predicated on a belief in something. Referring to the absence of self-sufficiency or substantiality in persons, emotions, or things, emptiness describes the lack of just those qualities of independence and individual identity that we so instinctually impute. Like the reflection in a rearview mirror, emptiness is not a thing in itself, yet it is nonetheless the vehicle for maintaining a proper view of the road in front of us.

The tendency of the human psyche, taught Nagarjuna, is either to reify or to deny, to impute absolute meaning or to impute none. Emptiness was his way of doing neither, of suspending judgment while still maintaining contact with the stuff of experience. It is as necessary for navigating our emotional terrain as the rearview mirror is for our travels on the highway, because when we attempt to drive without using the mirror, we get anxious, never knowing if it is safe to move to the left or right, or if someone is on our tail. When we operate with an appreciation of emptiness, teach the Buddhists, we are protected from the extremes of left and right (of grandiosity or despair), and when we are in danger of being overtaken by our own reactions to things, we can suddenly catch ourselves.

According to the Buddhist scholar Herbert Guenther, emptiness is the experience that "serves to destroy the idea of a persisting individual nature,"[6] but it is not an end in itself. It is especially useful in dealing with the thorny problem of the emotions, because a correct understanding of emptiness permits an alternative to the two extremes of emotional indulgence or emotional repression. As we practice meditation, we are forced to examine these coping strategies and to learn an alternative view.

HOLDING EMOTIONS

Emotional experience remains a problematic area for most people. We are all made uncomfortable by the intensity of our feelings, and we develop various ways of defending against this intensity. Buddhist emptiness is the key that unlocks the problem of the emotions. Emptiness is not hollow; it does not mean a vacuity of feeling. Emptiness is the understanding that the concrete appearances to which we are accustomed do not exist in the way we imagine, an experience that the late Tibetan lama Kalu Rinpoche called an "intangible" one, most comparable to that of "a mute person tasting sugar."[7] In particular, it means that the emotions that we take to be so real and are so worried about do not exist in the way we imagine them. They do exist, but we can *know* them in a way that is different from either expressing or repressing them. The Buddhist meditations on emptiness are not meant as a withdrawal from the falsely conceived emotions but as a means of *recognizing* the misconceptions that surround them, thereby changing the way that we experience them altogether. The Central Way of the Buddha has particular relevance in our emotional life.

One of the great lessons of the Fourth Noble Truth, and of the Buddha's teachings in general, is that it is possible to learn a new way to be with one's feelings. The Buddha taught a method of *holding* thoughts, feelings, and sensations in the balance of meditative equipoise so that they can be seen in a clear light. Stripping away the identifications and reactions that usually adhere to the emotions like moss to a stone, the Buddha's method allows the understanding of emptiness to emerge. This is an understanding that has vast implications for the field of psychotherapy because it promises great relief from even ordinary suffering. As the third Zen patriarch, writing in the early seventh century A.D., articulated with great clarity:

> *When the mind exists undisturbed in the Way,*
> *nothing in the world can offend,*
> *and when a thing can no longer offend,*
> *it ceases to exist in the old way. . . .*
> *If you wish to move in the One Way*
> *do not dislike even the world of senses and ideas.*
> *Indeed, to accept them fully*
> *is identical with true Enlightenment.*[8]

Training in this attitude of mind is why meditation is practiced.

PART II

MEDITATION

Then, the Licchavi Vimalakirti saw the crown prince Manjusri and addressed him thus: "Manjusri! Welcome, Manjusri! You are very welcome! There you are, without any coming. You appear, without any seeing. You are heard, without any hearing."

Manjusri declared, "Householder, it is as you say. Who comes, finally comes not. Who goes, finally goes not. Why? Who comes is not known to come. Who goes is not known to go. Who appears is finally not to be seen."

—Robert A. F. Thurman, *The Holy Teaching of Vimalakirti: A Mahayana Scripture*

THE RAFT

THERE IS no real word for meditation in the classical languages of Buddhism. The closest is one (*bhavana*) that translates best as something like "mental development." The lack of such a word is probably no accident, for it is not meditation, per se, that is important to the Buddha's psychology; it is the development of certain critical qualities of mind, beyond that which we accept as the norm, that is essential to the Buddha's teaching. In the Buddhist literature, for instance, there is a famous parable in which the Buddha describes a man going on a journey who fashions a raft out of grass, sticks, and leaves and branches in order to cross a great body of water that is blocking his path. It occurs to him, upon reaching the other shore, that the raft has been very useful to him, and he wonders if he should carry the raft with him just in case he should need it again.

> "What do you think, monks?" asks the Buddha. "That the man, in doing this, would be doing what should be done to the raft?"
> "No, lord."
> "What should that man do, monks, in order to do what should be done to that raft? In this case, monks, that man, when he has crossed over to the beyond and realizes how useful the raft has been to him, may think: 'Suppose that I, having beached this raft on dry ground, or having immersed it in the water, should proceed on my journey?' Monks, a man doing this would be doing what should be done to the raft. In this way, monks, I have taught you *dhamma*—the parable of the raft—for getting across, not for retaining. You, monks, by understanding the parable of the raft, must discard even right states of mind and, all the more, wrong states of mind."[1]

The raft of this story is meditation, permitting one to float where one would otherwise drown. The river is samsara, the Wheel of Life, the Six Realms of Existence, the mind, body, and emotions. Meditation, in this parable, is a method of mental development that permits us to traverse the waters of mind. This is a metaphor that the Buddha used time and again to describe the particular qualities of meditation that make it a useful vehicle for self-exploration. In the first text of the *Samyutta Nikaya* (Kindred Sayings), for example, the Buddha alludes to just this function of meditation:

> "How, Lord, did you cross the flood [of samsara]?"
> "Without tarrying, friend, and without struggling did I cross the flood."
> "But how could you do so, O Lord?"
> "When tarrying, friend, I sank, and when struggling, I was swept away. So, friend, it is by not tarrying and not struggling that I have crossed the flood."[2]

It is perhaps no accident that Freud, that great explorer of the watery depths of the unconscious, closed one of his only commentaries on an unnamed friend's experiments with yoga with a quote from Friedrich von Schiller's poem "The Diver." Freud used this poem to justify a hasty turning away from what his friend had described as an exploration of "primordial states of mind which have long ago been overlaid." Freud was uncharacteristically not intrigued by the idea of such an exploration. It was as if he feared drowning in the inchoate nature of his primitive mind. "Let him rejoice who breathes up here in the roseate light," quoted Freud, rejecting his friend's fascination with what Freud referred to as "a number of obscure modifications of mental life."[3] What Freud did not entirely grasp was that the meditative experience did not have to be a floundering in the deep but could, instead, be a floating across that did not require the holding of the breath. It is, in fact, one of the great similarities between meditation and psychoanalysis that both counsel this middle ground between tarrying and struggling as the most useful mental approach to one's own experience.

I am reminded of a time of self-retreat that I once engaged in some years ago along with one of my meditation teachers, Joseph Goldstein. After we broke silence and emerged from the several weeks of intensive practice, Joseph's first words, uttered with an air of bemused incredulity, were the following: "The mind has no pride." The double entendre was characteristic of Joseph's interpretation of Buddhist teachings: in a period of intensive meditation one sees many embarrassing things about oneself, but if one looks intently enough, one finds no one (no *thinker*) to be embarrassed by it all.

It is this combination of exploration, tolerance, and humor that has so impressed me in the experienced meditators that I have met. It is not a capacity that one finds at random, nor is it one that seems to grow predictably out of psychoanalysis alone.

CHAPTER 6

BARE ATTENTION

A T MY FIRST meditation retreat, a two-week period of silent attention to mind and body, I was amazed to find myself sitting in the dining hall with an instant judgment about each of the hundred other meditators, based on nothing besides how they looked while eating. Instinctively, I was searching out whom I liked and whom I did not: I had a comment for each one. The seemingly simple task of noting the physical sensations of the in and out breath had the unfortunate effect of revealing just how out of control my everyday mind really was.

Meditation is ruthless in the way it reveals the stark reality of our day-to-day mind. We are constantly murmuring, muttering, scheming, or wondering to ourselves under our breath: comforting ourselves, in a perverse fashion, with our own silent voices. Much of our interior life is characterized by this kind of primary process, almost infantile, way of thinking: "I like this. I don't like that. She hurt me. How can I get that? More of this, no more of that." These emotionally tinged thoughts are our attempts to keep the pleasure principle operative. Much of our inner dialogue, rather than the "rational" secondary process that is usually associated with the thinking mind, is this

constant reaction to experience by a selfish, childish protago-
nist. None of us has moved very far from the seven-year-old
who vigilantly watches to see who got more.

Buddhist meditation takes this untrained, everyday mind as
its natural starting point, and it requires the development of
one particular attentional posture—of naked, or bare, attention.
Defined as "the clear and single-minded awareness of what actually happens *to* us and *in* us at the successive moments of perception,"[1] bare attention takes this unexamined mind and opens
it up, not by trying to change anything but by observing the
mind, emotions, and body the way they are. It is *the* fundamental tenet of Buddhist psychology that this kind of attention is,
in itself, healing: that by the constant application of this attentional strategy, all of the Buddha's insights can be realized for
oneself. As mysterious as the literature on meditation can seem,
as elusive as the koans of the Zen master sometimes sound,
there is but one underlying instruction that is critical to Buddhist thought. Common to all schools of thought, from Sri
Lanka to Tibet, the unifying theme of the Buddhist approach is
this remarkable imperative: "Pay precise attention, moment by
moment, to exactly what you are experiencing, right now, separating out your reactions from the raw sensory events." This is
what is meant by bare attention: just the *bare* facts, an *exact* reg-
istering, allowing things to speak for themselves as if seen for
the first time, distinguishing any reactions from the core event.

DIMINISHING REACTIVITY

It is this attentional strategy that is followed throughout the
meditative path. It is both the beginning practice and the culminating one: only the objects of awareness change. Beginning

with the in and out breath, proceeding to bodily sensations, feelings, thoughts, consciousness, and finally the felt sense of I, meditation requires the application of bare attention to increasingly subtle phenomena. Culminating in a state of *choiceless awareness* in which the categories of "observer" and "that which is observed" are no longer operational, bare attention eventually obviates self-consciousness and permits the kind of spontaneity that has long intrigued the psychologically minded observers of Eastern practices. This is the spontaneity that Western psychologists confuse with a true self idea. From the Buddhist perspective, such authentic actions leap forth from the clear perception of bare attention; there is no need to posit an intermediate *agent* who performs them.

The key to the transformational potential of bare attention lies in the deceptively simple injunction to separate out one's reactions from the core events themselves. Much of the time, it turns out, our everyday minds are in a state of reactivity. We take this for granted, we do not question our automatic identifications with our reactions, and we experience ourselves at the mercy of an often hostile or frustrating outer world or an overwhelming or frightening inner one. With bare attention, we move from this automatic identification with our fear or frustration to a vantage point from which the fear or frustration is attended to with the same dispassionate interest as anything else. There is enormous freedom to be gained from such a shift. Instead of running from difficult emotions (or hanging on to enticing ones), the practitioner of bare attention becomes able to *contain* any reaction: making space for it, but not completely identifying with it because of the concomitant presence of nonjudgmental awareness.

A patient of mine illustrates this point directly. Temporarily abandoned by his mother at the age of six because of her nervous breakdown, Sid developed one obsessive love after another in his adult years, all with women with whom he had only brief affairs. He would pursue them relentlessly, calling them on the phone, writing them long, painful letters that spelled out how he had been misunderstood, and talking to them endlessly in his mind to explain his good intentions and to detail how he had been wronged. Each obsession lasted the better part of a year, and he rejected as unhelpful any interpretations I made about the feelings for these women being related to unexamined reactions from the time of his mother's unavailability. Our sessions would usually get no further than Sid repeating over and over again, "It hurts, it hurts." After many sessions such as this, I finally began to encourage Sid to go more deeply into his pain, to feel the hurt *and* all of his reactions to it without necessarily acting on it. There was no immediate breakthrough, but several months later, Sid appeared for his weekly session in an obviously less agitated state of mind.

"You know, something that you've been saying actually helped," he began. "'Just feel the pain,' you said. Well, the other night, instead of dialing Rachel's number, I decided to give it a try. And I decided, even if it kills me, that I would just lay there and feel the pain. And I did."

At that point, Sid looked at me in silence with a look that managed to convey both deep pain and triumph. He had begun to use bare attention to tame his mind. No longer driven to act out his pain by obsessively calling the women who he dreamed would assuage it, Sid managed to interrupt the behavior that was only perpetuating his isolation. In so doing, he began the process of accepting his own most difficult feelings. The paradox of bare attention, however, is that in this acceptance is a simultaneous letting go. The horror, or fear, at the pain that had made Sid run to these women for protection had only made the pain more intractable. Only by being with the emotions directly could Sid see them for what they were: old feelings, never fully experienced, that had conditioned his entire emotional life. By finding a way to be with those feelings without endlessly reacting to them, Sid was able to experience himself as something other than just a wrongfully rejected lover. He was making the shift from emotional reactivity to nonjudgmental awareness, not in the service of denial, repression, or suppression, but of growth and flexibility.

One famous Japanese haiku illustrates the state that Sid managed to discover in himself. It is one that Joseph Goldstein has long used to describe the unique attentional posture of bare attention:

> *The old pond.*
> *A frog jumps in.*
> *Plop!*[2]

Like so much else in Japanese art, the poem expresses the Buddhist emphasis on naked attention to the often overlooked details of everyday life. Yet, there is another level at which the poem may be read. Just as in the parable of the raft, the waters of the pond can represent the mind and the emotions. The frog jumping in becomes a thought or feeling arising in the mind or body, while "Plop!" represents the reverberations of that thought or feeling, unelaborated by the forces of reactivity. The entire poem comes to evoke the state of bare attention in its utter simplicity.

THE ART OF PSYCHOANALYSIS

Freud counseled a very similar state during the practice of psychoanalysis. He appears to have stumbled on it while analyzing his own dreams, making some use of a previous interest in the art of hypnosis. Freud makes reference to this particular deployment of attention throughout his writings, when he discusses the interpretation of dreams, free association, and "evenly suspended attention," the attentional stance that he recommends for practicing psychoanalysts.[3] There is no evidence that Freud was influenced directly by Buddhist practices, but the resemblance of his attentional recommendations to those of the Buddha cannot be denied.

Freud's major breakthrough, which he refers to over and over again in his writings, was his discovery that it was actually possible to suspend what he called the "critical faculty." This suspension of the critical faculty was, in fact, what made the practice of psychoanalysis possible for Freud. It is a feat that he accomplished with no outside help, one that he apparently taught himself without knowing that this was precisely the attentional stance that Buddhist meditators had been invoking for millennia.

Freud's writings on the subject reveal the first essential quality of bare attention—its impartiality. Repeatedly admonishing psychoanalysts to "suspend . . . judgement and give . . . impartial attention to everything there is to observe,"[4] Freud insisted that in this state it was possible to understand psychic phenomena in a unique fashion. While remaining interested in psychic *content*, he was nevertheless encouraging his followers to practice evenly suspended attention, a kind of beginning meditation. His instructions have all the clarity of those from the best Buddhist teachers. In his definitive article on the subject, Freud can be appreciated in his best Zenlike form:

The rule for the doctor may be expressed: "He should withhold all conscious influences from his capacity to attend, and

give himself over completely to his 'unconscious memory.'"
Or, to put it purely in terms of technique: "He should simply
listen, and not bother about whether he is keeping anything
in mind."[5]

This state of simply listening, of impartiality, is at once completely natural and enormously difficult. It is a challenge for
therapists to put aside their desires for a patient's cure, their
immediate conclusions about the patient's communications, and
their "insights" into the causes of the patient's suffering so that
they may continue to hear from the patient what they do not yet
understand. It is all the more challenging to turn this kind of
attention on oneself, as is required in meditation practice, to separate oneself from one's own reactions, to move from an identity
based on likes and dislikes to one based on impartial, nonjudgmental awareness. Bare attention requires the meditator to not
try to screen out the unpleasant, to take whatever is given.

OPENNESS

The next important quality of bare attention—openness—
grows out of this ability to take whatever is given. Requiring
the meditator to scan with a wide lens, not a narrow one, this
openness establishes a receptive intrapsychic environment for
exploration of the personal and private. It is the openness of a
mother who can, as D. W. Winnicott pointed out in his famous
paper "The Capacity to Be Alone," allow a child to play unin-
terruptedly in her presence.[6] This type of openness, which is
not interfering, is a quality that meditation reliably induces.

The late composer John Cage, heavily influenced as he was

by Buddhist philosophy, illustrates just this openness in his discussions of sound and music:

> If you develop an ear for sounds that are musical it is like developing an ego. You begin to refuse sounds that are not musical and that way cut yourself off from a good deal of experience. . . . The most recent change in my attitude toward sound has been in relation to loud sustained sounds such as car alarms or burglar alarms, which used to annoy me, but which I now accept and even enjoy. I think the transformation came through a statement of Marcel Duchamp who said that sounds which stay in one location and don't change can produce a sonorous sculpture, a sound sculpture that lasts in time. Isn't that beautiful?[7]

When we can develop this attitude toward our own internal car alarms, we can begin to feel the relevance of the Buddha's approach.

A patient who recently consulted with me had just this task facing him, because of his own version of the screeching alarms that made him want to shut down. Paul was the only child of an extraordinarily agitated and complaining mother whose husband had abandoned her when Paul was six. He had spent the better part of his preadolescent years alone in his house with his mother, sleeping in her bed and comforting her when she was down. He had remarkably few childhood memories, but he did recall his father having broken his favorite record because he would listen to it over and over again and cry to himself. As an adult, Paul was anxious and depressed much of the time and complained of not feeling real. He described himself as a "bundle of nerves" who was great at coping but felt no underlying excitement or confidence in what he was doing. He had a hard time saying what he felt anxious about, however, and a surprisingly difficult time exploring his discomfort in his first sessions with me.

He was afraid to look at his anxieties, he revealed: they reminded him of his mother's and made him feel as if he was as disturbed as she had seemed.

Paul's work in therapy was to learn to apply bare attention to his own anxiety, about which he knew very little. His first reaction was to be afraid and to clamp down on the anxiety. When he learned to isolate that initial reaction, to be with his fear, he was then able to distinguish *his* anxieties from those of his mother, and to realize that his parents had been unable to meet, or hold, those very feelings when they arose in him. Both psychotherapy and meditation had something basic to offer Paul: each in its own way could teach him how to be with his feelings without judging them the way his parents had. Only out of being with those actual feelings could Paul begin to gain some confidence in himself as a real person.

Bare attention requires an *openness* to both internal and sensory experience that does not often survive our childhoods. The child who is forced, as Paul was, to cope reactively with a parent's moods, loses touch with his or her own internal processes. Compelled to respond to the parent's needs, such a child relinquishes the ability to stay open to what necessarily seems less urgent, even if that is his or her own self. Thus, the false self is constructed and the narcissistic character, who does not really remember how to feel, is born.

By separating out the reactive self from the core experience, the practice of bare attention eventually returns the meditator to a state of unconditioned openness that bears an important resemblance to the feeling engendered by an optimally attentive parent. It does this by relentlessly uncovering the reactive self and returning the meditator, again and again, to the raw material of experience. According to Winnicott, only in this "state of not having to react" can the self "begin to be."[8]

ASTONISHMENT

As noted before, bare attention is impartial, nonjudgmental, and open. It is also deeply interested, like a child with a new toy. The key phrase from the Buddhist literature is that it requires "not clinging and not condemning," an attitude that Cage demonstrated with regard to the car alarms, that Winnicott described in his "good enough mothering" notion, that Freud counseled for the psychoanalyst at work, and that meditation practitioners must develop toward their own psychic, emotional, and physical sufferings. The most revealing thing about a first meditation retreat (after seeing how out of control our minds are) is how the experience of pain gives way to one of peacefulness if it is consistently and dispassionately attended to for a sufficient time. Once the reactions to the pain—the horror, outrage, fear, tension, and so on—are separated out from the pure sensation, the sensation at some point will stop hurting.

The psychoanalyst Michael Eigen, in a paper entitled "Stones in a Stream," describes his own first mystical experience in just these characteristic terms:

> I remember once being in emotional agony on a bus in my 20's. I doubled over into my pain and focused on it with blind intensity. As I sat there in this wretched state, I was amazed when the pain turned to redness, then blackness (a kind of blanking out), then light, as if a vagina in my soul opened, and there was radiant light. The pain did not vanish, but my attention was held by the light. I felt amazed, uplifted, stunned into awareness of wider existence. Of course I did not want the light to go away, and was a bit fearful that it would, but above all was reverence, respect: it could last as long as it liked, and come and go as it pleased. It was an unforgettable moment. Life can never be quite the same after such experiences.[9]

This kind of experience can truly come as a revelation. When we see that staying with a pain from which we habitually recoil can lead to such a transformation, it makes us question one of our basic assumptions: that we must reject that which does not feel good. Instead, we discover, even pain can be interesting.

OUR OWN MINDS

A further quality of bare attention, its unafraid nature, grows out of this interest. The psychiatrist R. D. Laing, at one of the first conferences on Buddhism and psychotherapy that I attended, declared that we are all afraid of three things: other people, our own minds, and death. His statement was all the more powerful because it came shortly before his own death. If bare attention is to be of any real use, it must be applied in exactly these spheres. Physical illness usually provides us with such an opportunity.

When my father-in-law, an observant Jew with little overt interest in Eastern philosophy, was facing radical surgery not so long ago, he sought my counsel because he knew of some work I was engaged in about stress reduction. He wanted to know how he could manage his thoughts while going into the surgery, and what he could do while lying awake at night? I taught him bare attention to a simple Jewish prayer; he was gradually able to expand the mental state that developed around the prayer to encompass his thoughts, anxieties, and fears. Even in the intensive care unit after surgery, when he could not tell day from night, move, swallow, or talk, he was able to use bare attention to rest in the moment, dissolving his fears in the meditative space of his own mind. Several years later, after attending Yom Kippur services, he showed me a particular passage in the prayer book that reminded him of what he had learned through his ordeal. A more Buddhist verse he could not have uncovered:

> A man's origin is from dust and his destiny is back to dust, at risk of his life he earns his bread; he is likened to a broken shard, withering grass, a fading flower, a passing shade, a dissipating cloud, a blowing wind, flying dust, and a fleeting dream.

The fearlessness of bare attention is necessary in the psychological venue as well, where the practice of psychotherapy has revealed just how ingenious and intransigent the ego's defenses can be. Even when they are in therapy, people are afraid of discovering things about themselves that they do not wish to know.

An accomplished artist named Maddie demonstrated this in a recent therapy session with me. "I don't want to be here," she declared. "I don't want to be your patient. I find it humiliating. I'd rather just be your friend." Maddie did not want to talk about the only topic she had to discuss with me therapeutically, namely, the way she made herself unapproachable with her lover. "It's the same with you as it is with her—it's too much work," she would say.

Somehow I was able to get Maddie to pay attention to her reluctance to being my patient. In turning it from an obstacle to a self-generated feeling, Maddie began to cry. This she found terribly embarrassing and curiously satisfying. Her impulse to cry, it seemed, was something that she was living in fear of. She had all kinds of voices in her head about it: crying was weak, unacceptable, inappropriate, humiliating, and not allowed, and any impulse to approach her lover was automatically stifled out of a fear of a similar breakdown with her. She had retreated to an angry, petulant, and defensive position; any attempt to reach out from this place evoked feelings of fear.

This fear is what, in psychoanalytic circles, is often called resistance. The fearlessness of bare attention must take this very fear as object: in contacting it, the patient can then become more real. In bare attention, the courage or fearlessness that can look at any manifestation of this insecurity is always combined with an equally strong patience or tolerance for that very feeling. Some psychoanalytic schools have made the mistake of relentlessly attacking the resistance, with the idea of releasing the underlying true self. This approach lacks the quality of tolerance that allows people to actually own their resistance, thereby evoking some grudging respect for their own involvement in creating it.

From a Buddhist perspective, there is really *nothing but* resistance to be analyzed; there is no true self waiting in the wings to be released. Only by revealing the insecurity can a measure of freedom be gained. When we can know our fear as fear and surround it with the patience of the Buddha, we can begin to rest in our own minds *and* approach those to whom we would like to feel close.

My use of bare attention with Maddie was applied with this in mind. It was necessary first to explore her defensive and angry posture and then her underlying fear and sadness. Maddie *was* her resistance: as she embodied it by becoming the angry, spiteful, frightened person who did not want to be my patient, she began to cry and experienced a *real* moment with me, about which she was deeply ashamed. At each level, the correct understanding of bare attention permitted her, in the words of the Buddha, not to tarry and not to struggle. As Maddie learned to be with her own feelings with the combination of courage and patience that bare attention requires, she became both more humble and more forthcoming, more capable of the intimacy that she both feared and craved.

*   *   *

TRANSITIONAL SPACE

The final quality of bare attention I want to emphasize is its impersonality. Like a stray dog that has no owner, the stray thoughts and feelings that are attended to with bare attention are treated as if they, too, are ownerless. This approach encourages a new version of what Winnicott called "transitional space." Long recognized as the crucial stepping-stone between infantile dependence and the ability to tolerate being alone, transitional space has been called an "intermediate area of experience"[10] that permits the child a feeling of comfort when separated from the parents. While Freud's famous equation of mysticism with the oceanic feeling has encouraged generations of psychoanalysts to see meditation as a shortcut to experiences of infantile narcissism, this formulation, at least in regard to bare attention, has clearly missed its mark. If therapists had recognized the similarity of meditative states to transitional phenomena, a clear link between Buddhism and psychoanalytic psychology would have been established long ago.

The transitional object—the teddy bear, stuffed animal, blanket, or favorite toy—makes possible the movement from a purely subjective experience to one in which other people are experienced as truly "other." Neither "me" nor "not-me," the transitional object enjoys a special in-between status that the parents instinctively respect. It is the raft by which the infant crosses over to the understanding of the other.

Many qualities of the transitional object—its ability to survive intense love and hate, its resistance to change unless changed by the infant, its ability to provide refuge and warmth, and its gradual relinquishment—are all shared by bare attention. Like the transitional object for the infant, bare attention enjoys a special status for the meditator: it, too, is an

in-between phenomenon. It is different from our usual subjective awareness and has been portrayed in the Tibetan tradition
as a kind of "spy consciousness" that observes from the corners
of the mind.

As an "observer," bare attention is reminiscent of the transitional object, since, like the infant's teddy bear, it is neither
"me" nor "not-me," but encompasses both. When meditators
hear a loud sound with bare attention, for example, they do not
distinguish the "hearer" from the "sound." Instead, there is only
the moment of "hearing," the coming together of internal and
external. In this moment of hearing, there is no inside and no
outside, just as it is impossible to say whether the breath comes
from within or without. This is not the only similarity. Like the
transitional object, bare attention can be a constant. Neither
intense emotion nor intense stimulation need disrupt it, because
its mirrorlike clarity can reflect whatever enters its field. An
image that is sometimes used to convey this constancy is that of
a stream rushing under a stone bridge. Through bare attention,
it is said, the meditator becomes not like the stream but like the
bridge with the stream rushing underneath.

Out of this constancy comes the ability to contain, or to
hold, experience. This is the counterpart to the infant's finding
warmth or solace in the transitional object and learning to hold
himself in the face of a newfound separateness. As the child
becomes comfortable with this separateness, he gradually relinquishes the transitional object. My eight-year-old daughter no
longer carries her teddy bear with her everywhere, but she does
still return to it at night. As the meditator becomes comfortable with applying bare attention, it too is gradually forgotten,
and the meditator is able to settle into choiceless awareness.

In making all of these comparisons, the essential point to
remember is that meditation is not transitional *in the same way*
as the infant's original object, which helped ease the transition

to separateness. Meditation picks up once separateness has been more or less achieved. It is transitional to something new: a state in which the reality of the separate self (and "real object") is called into question. By not identifying with, not holding on to, and not being embarrassed by whatever arises, the meditator moves inexorably from a narrow focus on the content of her experience to an ever-widening focus on the process itself. Thoughts and feelings, stripped of their associated pride or shame, gradually lose their charge and come to be seen as "just" thoughts or "just" feelings.

The transitional object that Winnicott described enables the infant to manage the intense feelings of desire and hatred that must inevitably be faced if the child is to come to terms with the realization that the parent is really an other and that the child, by implication, is really a self. The transitional space of meditation, on the other hand, helps one manage the troublesome emotions of the acquired self: pride, self-respect, conceit, outrage, the feelings that come when one's territory has been violated. This is not to say that simple hatred or greed will not show up in meditation or that meditators will not still, in some way, be dealing with primitive impulses such as rage or desire, but that the transitional space of meditation offers something different from that of the infant. Coming on the heels of the development of self (however fractured, insecure, or hollow that self may feel) and joined with the copresent factor of awareness, meditation offers a refuge where the fixed beliefs in a separate self that must be protected and defended can be temporarily suspended. The purpose is not only to create a safe resting place or a sense of ontological security, but to call into question the way we instinctively identify with our emotional responses.

There is an apparent contradiction with psychotherapy in this, one that has confounded more than a few therapists interested in the Buddhist perspective. From a psychoanalytic view, of course, a person must learn to see what has been disavowed and what is unconscious as, in fact, self-generated. In Freud's view, involuntary ideas or feelings must be transformed into voluntary ones: where id was, there ego must learn to be. From the Buddha's perspective, the very act of repossessing or of contacting one's own direct experience opens up the possibility of understanding the impersonality of that very experience. Taking it to that level is what the Buddha felt was necessary for real relief. His view is consistent with Freud's, yet it adds another dimension. Thoughts and emotions may be owned, the Buddha would agree, but unless there is the concomitant understanding that no "inherently existent" owner is present, the victory that Freud aspired to would be a Pyrrhic one.

THE POWER OF AWARENESS

Breaking identification through the power of awareness is the great contribution of the meditative approach, and it is inevitably therapeutic. Meditators often notice the therapeutic effects in surprising ways. An old friend of mine with years of meditative experience noticed it when she would visit her family. At first, when she would return home for a family dinner, she would find herself sitting around the table with her parents, brothers, and sisters, and she would notice a familiar and grossly uncomfortable feeling of invisibility, of not being appreciated for who she was. The next thing she knew, she would be in the kitchen furtively eating compulsively.

After years of training in meditation practice, however, this same woman made a similar visit home, noticed the same feelings arising at the dinner table, but stayed with them. She experienced her indignant expectation of attention from her family, the rage at their "withholding," the disappointment with herself for not being "good enough" to elicit their attention, and the terrible anxiety of sitting there not knowing what to do to change the situation. But she was not exclusively identified with these feelings. She could let them pass through her with some equilibrium, knowing that her awareness was strong enough to outlast the emotional upheaval. She did not have to eat compulsively, and she found that she was not waiting endlessly for the kind of attention that was never forthcoming. At some point, she remembers, she made a joke about the food, and she laughed with a force that startled her.

Meditation was helpful to my friend on two fronts. First, she was able to recognize and tolerate the disturbing cascade of expectation, righteous indignation, disappointment, insufficiency, and anger that had previously prompted her to eat compulsively. Second, she was able to release herself from the grip of this inadequacy, not by making it go away, but by knowing herself as something other than just this set of feelings. A more accurate Buddhist interpretation of this evolution might suggest that she knew herself as *nothing but* those feelings, but that she was able to experience their *emptiness* rather than being moved by their intrinsic reality. In any case, she felt more in control and less of a prisoner of her familial drama.

WISELY SEEING

Bare attention is the technique that best defines the Buddhist approach to working with our own minds and emotions. It is impartial, open, nonjudgmental, interested, patient, fearless, and impersonal. In creating a psychic space analogous to, but not identical with, Winnicott's transitional space of childhood, it facilitates the ability to transform psychic disturbances into objects of meditation, turning the proverbial threat into a challenge, and is therefore of immense psychotherapeutic benefit. There is no emotional experience, no mental event, no disavowed or estranged aspect of ourselves that cannot be worked with through the strategy of bare attention.

In the traditional descriptions of the progress of meditation, beginning practice always involves coming to terms with the unwanted, unexplored, and disturbing aspects of our being. Although we try any number of supposedly therapeutic maneuvers, say the ancient Buddhist psychological texts, there is but one method of successfully working with such material—by *wisely seeing* it. As Suzuki Roshi, the first Zen master of the San Francisco Zen Center, put it in a talk entitled "Mind Weeds":

> We say, "Pulling out the weeds we give nourishment to the plant." We pull the weeds and bury them near the plant to give it nourishment. So even though you have some difficulty in your practice, even though you have some waves while you are sitting, those waves themselves will help you. So you should not be bothered by your mind. You should rather be grateful for the weeds, because eventually they will enrich your practice. If you have some experience of how the weeds in your mind change into mental nourishment, your practice will make remarkable progress. You will feel the progress. You will feel how they change into self-nourishment. . . . This is how we practice Zen.[11]

This is the promise of bare attention and the great discovery of the Buddha. The relevance of this discovery to psychotherapy cannot be overstated, since, as every veteran of psychotherapy can attest, analysis can easily give understanding without relief. Meditation offers a method of recycling psychic pain, bringing about the very relief that is otherwise so elusive. This is the reason for its extraordinary appeal to those conversant with psychotherapy. Meditation offers a method of working with emotional material that may be implied in the best psychotherapy but that is rarely made explicit. The Buddha was a master at making the method explicit.

CHAPTER 7

THE PSYCHODYNAMICS
OF MEDITATION

WHATEVER THEIR similarities, meditation and psychotherapy are not the same. The identical person, engaged in either pursuit, will have vastly different experiences. Psychoanalytic psychotherapy tends to lead to experiences that reenact earlier and more formative emotional relationships so that the person's history can be, in effect, *reconstructed*. Buddhist meditation tends to intensify certain ego functions so that the sense of self is at once magnified and *deconstructed*. Psychotherapy often involves the creation of a narrative to explain a person's history, while meditation is a process of questioning the most basic metaphors that we use to understand ourselves. The most moving emotional experiences in therapy are those of the transference, in which it is revealed how earlier relationships are still shaping and defining present-day interactions, as demonstrated in the actual relationship with the therapist. The most moving experiences in meditation are those that enable the meditator to come face-to-face with various cherished images of self, only to reveal how ultimately lacking such images are.

Much of what happens through meditation is therapeutic, in that it promotes the usual therapeutic goals of integration, humility, stability, and self-awareness. Yet there is something in the scope of Buddhist meditation that reaches beyond therapy, toward a farther horizon of self-understanding that is not ordinarily accessible through psychotherapy alone. Whereas psychoanalysis takes the therapeutic relationship and cultivates it through the power of the therapist's analytic attitude, meditation takes actual qualities of mind and cultivates them internally so that the person's powers of observation are increased. With these increased contemplative powers, the meditator is then able to scan and to hold what can best be described as the building blocks of self-experience, the basic cravings that give rise to the sense of self. In so doing, one's deeply ingrained sense of self is profoundly and irrevocably transformed.

The difference in these two methods can best be described through the following examples. An accomplished woman and experienced meditator who had had a horrendous childhood, Jean came to me for therapy for what she called "relationship problems." After about a year of therapy, in which she could talk intelligently about a wide range of both spiritual and psychological issues, it became obvious that, in some way, Jean was avoiding me. At the same time, she began to speak of a feeling of disappointment in the therapy, of not getting what she thought she wanted from it, but of being unsure about exactly what that was. Shortly thereafter, a most moving encounter unfolded. As I pursued my sense of being avoided and her doubts about the therapy, Jean had the sudden sense of actively keeping me from being important to her. "If I care about you, you will leave," she blurted out, connecting me immediately to every important figure from her past who had done just that. With that realization, we could then begin to work on *how* Jean managed to keep herself from caring for someone, using the often treacherous material of the transference as a laboratory to examine the details up close. This was doing what therapy does best—enabling Jean to see how she was unconsciously reproducing behavior that had once been adaptive but was now simply repetitive, using the relationship with the therapist to demonstrate her unaware inhibition of herself.

Meditation, on the other hand, especially in its more developed forms, is often much less specific in its focus. When one begins to practice meditation, psychological issues usually predominate. But as the practices of concentration, mindfulness, and analytic insight are developed, the psychodynamics change, and the emotional issues of one's childhood often retreat as the focus shifts to an examination of *how* one experiences oneself. Sometimes, meditators need to come back to the psychological level to work on a specific problem. Jean had had extensive meditative experiences. For example, she had uncovered much grief, pain, and loss, and she had experienced blissful and soothing states that had vastly reassured her about the vitality of her being. She had not, however, come face-to-face in her meditative work with her avoidance of caring feelings. Deep meditation is much more generic than psychotherapy: it is less about the individual details of a person's history and more about the fundamental predicaments of being. The focus moves from *what* is being repeated to *who* it is that needs to repeat.

TERROR AND DELIGHT

One of the best descriptions of the actual psychological experiences that come with deep meditation is the *Visuddhimagga* (Path of purification), a fourth-century meditation manual composed on the island of Sri Lanka by an Indian Buddhist named Buddhaghosa. In the *Visuddhimagga* he laid out the early Buddhist vision of what can be achieved psychologically through the cultivation of certain critical factors of mind that are developed through meditation practice. As a cross section of the meditative mind, this manual is unparalleled. Through the relentless development of both concentration (the ability to rest the mind in a single object of awareness) and mindfulness (the ability to shift attention to a succession of objects of awareness), the meditator eventually enters into states that are variously described as ones of either *terror* or *delight*. These are states that do not often unfold in psychotherapy: they may be glimpsed or remembered, but they do not come forward inexorably, as they do in meditation practice. Their emergence is predicated on the development of certain ego functions beyond the normal operating range of everyday life.

Listen, for example, to the classic descriptions of some of these states. The experiences of delight, for instance, are characterized by varying degrees of rapture or happiness, of which there are said to be five grades:

> *Minor happiness* is only able to raise the hairs on the body. *Momentary happiness* is like flashes of lightning at different moments. *Showering happiness* breaks over the body again and again like waves on the seashore. *Uplifting happiness* can be powerful enough to levitate the body and make it spring up in the air. . . . But when *pervading (rapturous) happiness* arises, the whole body is completely pervaded, like a filled bladder, like a rock cavern invaded by a huge inundation.[1]

The experiences of terror, on the other hand, tend to reveal just how precarious the sense of self actually is, and just how groundless the soil of narcissistic craving can be. They have the effect of pulling the rug out from under us, of shaking the foundation on which we have constructed our accepted vision of ourselves. They are experiences of a completely different caliber from those of delight, as can be seen in the following description from the same text:

> As he repeats, develops and cultivates in this way the contemplation of dissolution, . . . then formations . . . appear to him in the form of a great terror, as lions, tigers, leopards, bears, hyaenas, spirits, ogres, fierce bulls, savage dogs, rut-maddened wild elephants, hideous venomous serpents, thunderbolts, charnel grounds, battle fields, flaming coal pits, etc., appear to a timid man who wants to live in peace. When he sees how past formations have ceased, present ones are ceasing, and those to be generated in the future will cease, in just the same way, then what is called Knowledge of Appearance as Terror arises in him at that stage.[2]

What Westerners often do not understand is that experiences such as these require an ego, in the psychoanalytic sense, that is capable of holding and integrating what would ordinarily be violently destabilizing. One is challenged to experience terror without fear and delight without attachment. The work of meditation, in one sense, is the work of developing an ego that is flexible, clear, and balanced enough to enable one to have such experiences.

From another perspective, the work of meditation is to confront the attachments that make such an ego impossible to achieve. Invariably, these attachments are narcissistic ones. As meditation unfolds, the coarser aspects of the self, as personified by emotional upheaval or by the chattering mind, tend to become quieter, but more subtle attachments or identifications become visible in their stead. In this sense, meditation becomes rather like a labyrinth, with each new opening and each new perception about the self revealing yet another opportunity for attachment and release. What the meditator must keep confronting is her own capacity for conceit or pride, her own instinctive thirst for certainty, her own ability to co-opt the meditative process for narcissistic ends. Meditation is a means of indefatigably exposing this narcissism, of highlighting every permutation of the self-experience so that no aspect remains available for narcissistic recruitment.

Meditators, at every stage, tend to use their experiences and insights in a manner that reinforces their own sense of specialness, and the meditative path actually consists of continually uncovering and resolving those impulses by encouraging the meditator to always examine *where* they are most identified. When I had my first experience of showering happiness in meditation, for example, I was ecstatic. I thought something very impressive had occurred. The real opportunity of that experience, however, turned out to be for me to see my belief in my own specialness—to experience that, too, as an evanescent feeling. As this process repeats itself, the chronic ways that we think of and feel about ourselves are altered: the metaphors that we unconsciously use to understand ourselves are forced into question.

BEGINNING MEDITATION: SPLITTING THE EGO

Because preliminary meditation practices are in many ways more closely related to psychotherapy than are other practices along the meditative path, they often are the most difficult for beginning students to navigate successfully. The similarities can be both overpowering and seductive, and many a "psychologically minded" meditator has labored intensively, trying to "do therapy" while appearing to be meditating. Since meditation and psychotherapy both require a therapeutic split in the ego, it can often be confusing *which* process to actually engage in. The observing ego, that which engages in bare attention or free association, is, after all, strengthened in meditation practice.

One psychoanalyst whom I know described his first meditation retreat after having undergone five years of psychoanalysis. At the retreat he felt that he understood for the first time what it meant to free-associate. The process of repeatedly applying bare attention strengthens the observing ego to a point where free association is really possible, he found. This discovery is often so rewarding that, from the viewpoint of the meditative path, bare attention is often not developed *past* the point of free association. But meditation eventually requires something other than a chain of mental and emotional associations, however intriguing or alarming those associations are, and however important for a successful psychotherapy they may be.

When the psychologists Daniel Brown and Jack Engler studied experienced meditators, they found, to their surprise, that meditators were just as anxious as everyone else. There was no lessening of internal conflict, but only a "marked non-defensiveness in experiencing such conflicts"[3] among their subjects. The implications of these findings are profound, because Brown and Engler discovered that meditation, on its own, is not particularly effective at solving people's emotional problems. It can prepare the ground, so to speak, by making the person more accepting and less defensive, but without a therapist's intervention, there is a very real danger of paralysis. We are faced here with our first conundrum: Meditation, it seems, can bestow the kind of ego strength necessary for a successful psychotherapy, but it cannot do the psychotherapy by itself. As discussed in part III, meditation can also rescue a psychotherapy, by providing the means of what Freud called "working-through," but this can happen only after the therapy has been established.

DWELLING IN THE PAIN

More often than not, a beginning meditation experience—by which I mean a first exploration of intensive practice—brings out what can best be described as a kind of primitive longing. At root, it is a longing for completeness, although the individual contents would, of course, vary with individual histories. My patient Jean, for example, whom I discussed at the beginning of this chapter, felt this longing primarily as a yearning for a satisfying relationship. It is this longing that often requires therapeutic attention, for any attempt by the meditator to solve the problem through fantasy, catharsis, or rumination will only prolong the previously mentioned state of paralysis. Jean spent many months coming up against this yearning before she had the courage to seek therapeutic help; others spend much longer.

From the Buddhist perspective, this longing is important because of how *identified* the meditator can be with this state. "Who is the self that longs?" the Buddhist teacher will repeatedly inquire. The problem for many Western meditators is that this approach to the problem is simply too impersonal at first. The psychic pain revealed at this stage and personified by the strong longing is often so central and so deeply personal that meditators can never let go of the wish that the meditation itself would magically heal them. It is far better that they seek therapeutic help at this stage rather than languishing in the netherworld of their own imaginations, secretly trying to break through their pain via meditation practice while, in fact, merely dwelling in their own longing.

The Buddha spoke obliquely of this tendency in his teachings of the Middle Path in which he counseled against the search for happiness through self-mortification. Such ascetic practices, he warned, are counterproductive. Many Western students of meditation, in their embrace of practice, lock themselves into a contemporary version of what the Buddha warned against by denying themselves needed therapeutic attention and, instead, feeling that they can "do it themselves" through their meditations. Shunning psychotherapy, they are nevertheless stuck in surreptitiously using meditation for psychotherapeutic purposes. As the Buddha said of the ascetic practitioners of his own age, they are like the blind leading the blind.

With Jean, meditation alerted her to the need for psychotherapy. She sought that out, learned how she was keeping caring feelings at bay, and did not get bogged down in grappling with her sense of unworthiness in the privacy of her own meditation. Many others do not make this transition so seamlessly: they become enamored of the observing self that beginning meditation empowers and use that capacity for self-observation as a way to avoid personal responsibility. They observe their own pain, but not their contribution to its making.

UNCOVERING THE SPATIAL METAPHOR

When we first undertake meditation practice, the underlying operating premises about the nature of our own selves almost always involve a spatial metaphor. This is also true in most beginning psychotherapies. We all tend to think about the self as Freud did, in spatial terms: as an entity with boundaries, layers, and a core, much like an onion or a building or an archaeological dig. "The mind is a place where things happen," says the psychoanalyst Stephen A. Mitchell of this view. "The self is something in this place, which is composed of constituent parts or structures."[4] One of the consequences of this mode of experiencing is that it feeds the tendency to search for a "core" or a true self at the "center" of our being. Another consequence can be seen in the longing for "wholeness" that is so common among those beginning both psychotherapy or meditation. Only when the self is conceived in spatial terms can this yearning for wholeness seem so compelling.

In beginning meditation practice, spatial metaphors predominate. The ego is "split," with the observing self practicing awareness of "objects" of mind and body. The mind is often experienced as a vast space within which flourish the various parts of the self, as a cave that must be penetrated, or as a plant that must be traced back to its roots. Beginning meditators often confront a feeling of hollowness or emptiness, coupled with a longing for completion or wholeness. This is usually a sign, in psychodynamic terms, of some estranged or disclaimed aspect of themselves that must be integrated through therapeutic endeavors. Here, too, the primary operating metaphor remains a spatial one that carries with it a subtle belief in the "thingness" of self, in the possibility of finding the core, the root, the center, or one's "true" identity. Meditation takes this spatial metaphor as a starting point and then begins to toy with it, teasing it gently at first, like a cat with a ball of string, but eventually exploding it with the concentrated intensity of what the psychologist and writer Daniel Goleman has called the "meditative mind."[5] In fact, the distinguishing characteristic of Buddhist meditation is that it seeks to eradicate, once and for all, the conception of self as an entity. In various critical ways, the three major meditative strategies—concentration, mindfulness, and insight—all work to this end.

RIGHT CONCENTRATION: EXPLORING THE SPATIAL METAPHOR

In his Eightfold Path, the Buddha spoke specifically about cultivating two particular kinds of attention: concentration and mindfulness. They are not the same. Traditionally, concentration is taught first. By repeatedly returning one's attention to a central object of awareness—a word, a sound, a sensation, a visual image, or an idea—feelings of tranquility are generated in mind and body. The chattering, discursive mind is quieted, and the experiences of delight begin to unfold. Yet, in the traditional Buddhist psychologies, these experiences are treated primarily as side effects of the concentration practices. They are repeatedly warned against because of their seductive powers, and yet the development of concentration is nevertheless encouraged and pursued. Why?

The answer lies in the power of the concentration practices to alter the spatial metaphors of the sense of self. There is nothing that characterizes developed states of one-pointedness as much as the dissolution of ego boundaries and feelings of merger, union, and oneness with the universe that led Freud to call these *oceanic* experiences. Psychodynamically, they certainly represent a kind of *ideal* experiencing, but this is decidedly not the function that the Buddhist theorists envision them playing. Rather, the concentration practices begin to break down the conception of self as an entity that we all hold.

In my teacher Jack Kornfield's early days as a celibate monk, for example, his experience was almost entirely defined by this spatial metaphor. Overwhelmed with sexual fantasies, Jack learned to apply bare attention to them and discovered not only that he was filled with desire but also that "a deep well of loneliness" came whenever the fantasies arose. As he dwelled more and more on the loneliness, he came to experience it as a "central hole" of longing, hunger, and inadequacy that he had been afraid to experience fully. Staying with those feelings, instead of trying to shut them down, he found that this central hole would expand and contract, eventually opening into a vast space of clear light that became a metaphor for an identity not limited by shame and insecurity.[6]

The spatial metaphor is a constant thread throughout Jack's account. Troubled at first by obsessive thoughts that he wished to disavow, he then discovered that they were linked to a "deep well" of loneliness. This was Jack's version of the hollowness or yearning that often characterizes early meditative experiences and that reinforces the ingrained notions of self as a *thing* that needs to be made whole. Looking closer into the "center," Jack peeled away the "layers" to discover the "central hole," which then was allowed to expand into "open space," releasing him from the attachment to his "contracted" view of himself.

This is by no means a unique report: it is quite literally the definition of what the concentration practices are capable of. They take the spatial view of self as empty, hollow, incomplete, or closed and expand it to infinity, allowing the meditator to rest in clear and open space. In advanced concentration practices, the body actually disappears: there are no physical sensations, only subtle sensations of joy, bliss, and open space. In yet more advanced states, even the subtle feelings of joy and bliss disappear, leaving only the sensations of space. Yet this is by no means the end point of Buddhist meditation. Such a practice certainly loosens the spatial notions of self, and the areas of fear, such as Jack's unworthiness, that reinforce a spatial metaphor of self can be relaxed and expanded. But there remains a compelling feeling of self as some vast space, linked perhaps to a universal or underlying mind that permeates all things. The spatial metaphor is ultimately preserved, and the meditator is vulnerable to the kind of grandiosity that the Buddha warned against in his Second Noble Truth. The task of the meditator upon developing Right Concentration is to see the limitation of even this expanded view of self, to recognize the appeal of hiding out in the ineffable or in vast open space and to turn away from the suffering that the attachment to such states entails.

From the point of view of Buddhist practice, the reason for developing concentration is to quiet the mind sufficiently to allow inquiry into the nature of self. The self-states that are discovered along the way provide opportunities to examine the hold that such idealized experiences can have over us. Yet, like the person who yearns for sexual activity, only to discover that it cannot bestow lasting happiness, the meditator who has yearned for wholeness finds that even its acquisition does not offer release.

RIGHT MINDFULNESS: EXPLORING THE TEMPORAL METAPHOR

One of the distinguishing marks of the Buddha's teachings was his repeated emphasis on the importance of mindfulness. Familiar, as he was, with techniques of concentration and one-pointedness and the experiences of delight that derive from their practice, the Buddha made it quite clear that these practices were not sufficient for his purposes. He taught that one must not escape into the concentrated absorption of the tranquil mind but rather contemplate what he called the "Four Foundations of Mindfulness," particularly the body, the feelings, the mind, and the thoughts and emotions, which he called "mental objects" or "mental factors." Like bare attention, mindfulness means being aware of exactly what is happening in the mind and body *as* it is occurring: what it reveals is how much of a flux we are in at all times.

Time

With the mindfulness practices comes a shift from a spatially based experience of self to a temporal one. Having accomplished a certain amount of inner stability through concentration, the meditator is now able to look more closely at the moment-to-moment nature of mind and self. Mindfulness involves awareness of how constantly thoughts, feelings, images, and sensations shift in the mind and body. Rather than promoting a view of self as an entity or as a place with boundaries, the mindfulness practices tend to reveal another dimension of the self-experience, one that has to do with how patterns come together in a temporary and ever-evolving organization.

This progression from a spatial metaphor of self to a more temporal one is portrayed in the Buddhist literature as inexorable. Once mindfulness has been developed, the self can never be thought of in the same spatially based manner again. Mindfulness is seen as the pivotal ingredient, the catalyst for a profound change in the way self is experienced. As one of the Buddha's chief disciples, Anuruddha, put it in a talk he gave to a convocation of monks in the Buddha's time:

This river here, the Ganges, brethren, flows to the East, is bent toward the East, directed toward the East. Now suppose a large group of people approaches, carrying mammoties and baskets, and they say: "We shall make this river, the Ganges, flow to the West, bend it toward the West, direct it toward the West." What do you think, brethren: can this large group of people actually make the Ganges flow toward the West, bend it toward the West, direct it toward the West?

—Verily not, brother.

—And why not?

—The Ganges, to be sure, brother, flows to the East, is bent toward the East, is directed toward the East. Impossible it is to make it flow to the West, to bend and direct it toward the West, whatever fatigue and pain this large group of people might undergo.

—Similarly, brethren: if a monk who has cultivated and frequently practiced the four Foundations of Mindfulness is surrounded by kings and ministers, by his friends, acquaintances and relatives and, offering treasure, they entreat him: "Come, my dear man! What do you want with these yellow robes? Why do you go about with a shaven head? Come, return to the lay life where you may enjoy your treasure and do good deeds!" But, brethren, that a monk who has cultivated and frequently practiced the four Foundations of Mindfulness, should give up the training and return to a lower state, this is not possible. And why not? There is no possibility that a mind turned for a long time toward detachment, directed toward detachment, should return to a lower state."[7]

As the shift from a spatially based sense of self to a temporally based one occurs, it becomes impossible to ignore just how removed we all are from what Mitchell has called the "rushing fluidity"[8] of our everyday experience. In the premindfulness state, our minds are most often operating independently of our bodies, on a different level, as it were, from the actions that our bodies are performing. When I read a bedtime story to my children, for instance, I can, at the same time, be plotting out the details of my next writing project to myself. If one of my children interrupts me to ask a question, I find that I have no idea what I am reading about. Rather than being mindful, I am instead reading mindlessly, and while I would prefer to think otherwise, my children's experience of me will be lifeless. Similarly, when walking to the store, washing the dishes, brushing our teeth, or even making love, we often are split off from our physical experience: we are quite literally not present. Our minds and bodies are not functioning as one.

Body

By emphasizing the mindfulness practices as he did, the Buddha pointed to the importance of remedying the splits that the spatially based metaphor of self encourages. When we think of our bodies as "things" that are separate from us and our minds as "places" where we think, we foster our own sense of alienation or remove. Mindfulness practice begins, for this reason, with awareness of the breath and the body: the appreciation of the temporally based dimension of self stems from the ability to pay attention to bodily based experiences *as they occur.* It is quite literally a coming to one's senses.

The British psychoanalyst Marion Milner, famous for her explorations of art and culture, gives a particularly vivid description of her own discovery of the power of mindfulness in her book *The Suppressed Madness of Sane Men.* Sitting in a garden at a residential art school in 1950 and struggling to find a subject to paint, she began to focus her attention on her breathing in order to deal with the frustration of the situation. Suddenly, she found that her experience of the world around her became quite transformed and "exceedingly paintable." She explains:

"It seemed odd, then, that turning one's attention inwards, not to awareness of one's big toe but to the inner sensations of breathing, should have such a marked effect on the appearance and significance of the world, but I had not yet thought of this in terms of mysticism."[9] And yet, Milner was subsequently to realize that this exercise of attention to her breathing had allowed her to let go of the habitual modes of perception that so define the conventional view of self.

Milner became preoccupied with bodily experience and its relationship with creativity after her episode in the garden, and she began to describe the connection between bodily based experience, the experience of vitality or aliveness, and a view of self that is conditioned by time, as opposed to space. As the Buddhist perspective confirms, opening to the transitoriness of experience paradoxically makes us feel more real.

Breath

Awareness of breathing and bodily sensations is probably the most fundamental Buddhist meditation practice. Before mindfulness can be successfully applied to feelings, thoughts, emotions, or mind, it must be firmly grounded in the awareness of breath and body. From a psychodynamic perspective, this is undoubtedly no accident, because awareness of breathing provides a unique opportunity for one to integrate time into the self experience. The usual psychodynamic foundation for the self experience is that of hunger, not breath. When this is the case, the body is experienced as an alien entity that has to be kept satisfied, the way an anxious mother might experience a new baby. When awareness is shifted from appetite to breath, the anxieties about not being enough are automatically attenuated. Just as a nursing mother learns to trust that her body will respond to her infant with milk, so meditators who shift to a breath-based foundation learn to surrender into the ebb and flow of their own breath. It requires a settling down or relaxing into one's own body. As the psychoanalyst Michael Eigen has noted:

> The sense of self based on a normal experience of breathing is an unpressured sense of self which is not easily stampeded. For the sense of self structured by appetite, time is an irritant. The self structured by an awareness of breathing can take its time going from moment to moment, just as breathing usually does. It does not run after or get ahead of time but, instead, seems simply to move with it.[10]

In Buddhist meditation, this progression from space to time, and from appetite to breath, is a given. Not content to simply demonstrate how cut off from our bodily experiences we are, the Buddha taught intensive mindfulness practice as a means of actually dissolving the perceived splits between mind and body, subject and object, and awareness and its objects. After quieting the mind, developing the observing ego, and approaching some sense of wholeness or open space, the emphasis shifts to an appreciation of just how difficult, and yet possible, it is to surrender to the flow of experience. Gradually expanding the foundations of mindfulness to include feelings, thoughts, emotions, and mind, the successful practitioner keeps coming up against her own desires to somehow halt the flow, to convert the breath-based experience of fluidity and change to an appetite-based one of gratification or satisfaction.

Yet just as the Buddha's disciple described, it is impossible to turn the river around. Once mindfulness is developed, there is no avoiding the relentless and teeming rush that underlies our experience. There comes a point in the intensive cultivation of mindfulness when it proceeds effortlessly and unencumbered, when experience unfolds continuously with awareness, but without self-consciousness. When this fluidity moves to the forefront of awareness, the appetite-based self of frustrations and gratifications recedes. There is a relaxation of the tensed self that evolved to manage parental intrusiveness or neglect and an emergence of a simpler, breath-based self that is capable of surrender to the moment.

Surrender

It is through the mindfulness practices that Buddhism most clearly complements psychotherapy. The shift from an appetite-based, spatially conceived self preoccupied with a sense of what is lacking to a breath-based, temporally conceived self capable of spontaneity and aliveness is, of course, one that psychotherapy has also come to envision. It is one of the most significant paradigm shifts to have taken root in psychoanalytic theory in recent years and is one of the reasons why the Buddha's message is now so appealing to the therapeutic community. As the old models are laid to rest, the Buddha's words become easier to comprehend. In fact, contemporary psychologists can start to sound suspiciously Buddhist when they compare the nature of self to that of a river or stream.

Mindfulness practice offers a direct route to appreciating the temporal nature of self. It is a force that the Buddha recognized and taught, but one that is not specifically tapped in most of today's psychotherapies. Yet, it is the most specific way of encouraging the self-awareness that Milner, Eigen, and Mitchell all describe as essential. As psychotherapy and meditation begin to come together, it is this function of mindfulness that will prove pivotal, because mindfulness permits continual surrender into our direct experience, from which we have all become experts at keeping ourselves at bay.

Let me offer something of a personal example of what I mean. When our first child was born, I took great pride in my ability to take care of her. As in most other aspects of my life, my capacity for efficiency was a priority for me. I had been raised to be capable and responsible and had come to enjoy making difficult tasks look easy; and parenting, although a different kind of challenge, was not immune to my means of approaching the world. After the first two months of our daughter's life, we took a trip to the country, to a small Buddhist monastery where friends were gathering for a morning of meditation and an afternoon of walking in the woods. Upon emerging from my morning of meditation and returning to my daughter, I was, for a moment, free of my compulsion to prove my efficiency, free of my ingrained habits of duty and obligation. She did, however, need to have her diaper changed, and my wife and I took her into the bathroom to do this. As we finished fussing over her, she looked up at us and smiled, giving us a look of such love that I immediately felt tears spring to my eyes. It was the first time that I had noticed her love coming back at me. I could have gone on for a very long time being efficient, I am sure, without ever noticing that look, yet because of my momentary ability to be more directly with my own sensory experience, I was able to receive my daughter's overture.

My ability, in that moment, to surrender my attachment to my own efficiency is an example of what mindfulness practice does best. It is this ego function of *surrender* that is most specifically developed in advanced states of mindfulness practice. As the Buddha taught in his Second Noble Truth, the cause of suffering is thirst. As mindfulness progresses, the meditator is consistently put in the position of seeing how strongly his own thirst, in the form of desire or aversion, threatens to disrupt the ongoing flow of consciousness. When I am in the middle of a particularly delicious mouthful of food, for example, I can see my desire to move another helping into my mouth as the flavor fades, before I have finished chewing and swallowing. I do not want to experience the fading of the flavor—the colorless, cottony pulp that succeeds that spectacular burst over my taste buds. It is the same in meditation practice: the oscillation between pleasurable and unpleasurable moments only becomes more vivid as mindfulness develops. The hunger-based, spatially conceived self continuously rubs up against its breath-based, temporally conceived cousin. The counsel of Buddhist teachers during intensive practice is always to surrender the individual will to the ongoing flow, to "let go," or, in the words of the Buddhist teacher Joseph Goldstein, "not to hold on."[11] Attachment is continuously surrendered as the meditator opens more and more to direct experience.

This is a particularly powerful time in meditation, for there is in most of us a profound longing for just this kind of giving up of the constraints of our personalities.[12] In mindfulness practice, this yielding of false self is a continual possibility. When I relinquished my need for efficient management of my infant daughter and caught her look of love, I had, for the moment, surrendered what D. W. Winnicott would have surely called my false self. When I permit myself to taste the faded remnants of a mouthful of food, I am, in a different way, surrendering my need for continual pleasure and opening to an authentic appreciation of my actual situation, not some fantasy of constant gratification that I am compelled to chase after until I make myself sick.

As the appetite-based self loses its strength, one's inner sense of aliveness or vitality seems to expand. Although there is a movement away from thirst, the resultant state is not without its charms. There is a parallel in the ancient myth of Psyche, which the psychoanalyst Jessica Benjamin recounts,[13] in which Psyche, though universally admired for her beauty, feels as if she were dead. Carried by the wind and deposited in a bed of flowers, Psyche is left to "awaken in a state of benign aloneness" in which she is freed from idealization and objectification so that she can finally await her lover, Eros. Like Psyche, the meditator practicing mindfulness must surrender her psyche to the winds that carry her, relinquishing the identifications that are based on idealization and objectification, the false self of narcissism that has led her to feel hollow or empty. Only in the resultant state of aloneness can vitality or aliveness, the force of Eros, emerge. This life force, personified in the myth by Eros, represents what Benjamin has called a deepening "subjectivity" that is pursued through psychotherapy and unleashed in meditation. Another way of understanding mindfulness practice, in fact, in the language of today's psychoanalysis, is as a way of "healing a disordered subjectivity"[14]: providing a method of being with one's own experience that is simple, direct, and immediate without the usual distortions of attachment and aversion that regularly color one's perceptions.

Indeed, in the traditional Buddhist descriptions of the progress of meditation, the practice of mindfulness culminates in an experience of Eros that has been called pseudonirvana because of its seductiveness. A charged state in which heightened awareness, sublime happiness, effortless energy, the vision of a brilliant light or luminous form, rapturous and devotional feelings, and profound tranquility and peace of mind all arise together, this state is the natural outgrowth of the repeated application of mindful awareness. It is called pseudonirvana because of the meditator's instant belief that *this* is the enlightened state. But it is, of course, not so simple. The deepening of subjectivity, the capacity for real and authentic relatedness, the awakening or revitalization of the life force, and the change in the mode of self-experiencing from a spatial to a temporal metaphor all are only stepping stones toward an actual intuitive understanding of emptiness, in the Buddhist sense. The rush of feeling and the unconflicted subjective awareness that emerge from the steady application of mindfulness are therapeutically very desirable, but they, too, can become the vehicles for narcissistic attachment.

The higher experiences of meditation are all basically ways of tricking the self into revealing more and more basic identifications, of evoking more and more delectable states that urge the feeling of "Ahhh, this is the real me!" out of us. In states of developed concentration the body disappears, even an emotion so coarse and disruptive as joy can disappear, but still there remains a feeling of pride or accomplishment. In mindfulness practice, self is experienced as a flow, a process, a rushing and teeming patterning that changes over time. A quiet mind free of thoughts, continual surrender into the moment, and relaxation of the constraints of false self all give the illusion of release from neurotic attachment. Yet these experiences, too, can become the basis for pride and attachment. The three objects of craving that the Buddha spoke about in his Second Noble Truth—sense pleasures, existence, and nonexistence—all are re-created in crystalline form in the progress of meditation so that the grasping after them can be identified. It is this grasping that the Buddha identified as the eradicable source of suffering, and meditation is designed to make this grasping familiar in all of its forms.

INSIGHT: EXPLORING THE METAPHOR OF SELF

Despite all of its sophistication—or, perhaps, because of it—"self" has remained a thorny issue in Western psychoanalytic psychology. But it is addressed head-on in Buddhism in critical analytic or insight (*vipassana*) meditation, in which the practices are distinct from both concentration and mindfulness exercises. Defined explicitly by the types of questions—such as Who am I? What is the true nature of self? What was your face before you were born?—this form of meditation requires the preliminary cultivation of both concentration and mindfulness as the foundation or structure that permits successful self-inquiry. Generations of psychoanalytic theorists have been preoccupied with these questions of the nature of self, which are also often the motivating forces for people who enter psychotherapy or meditation. Yet, psychotherapy has had trouble providing a satisfactory answer for the problem of self. All too often, psychoanalysts have been subject to the same rudimentary habits of thought in formulating their theories as are those beginning a meditation practice. As the interpersonal psychiatrist Harry Stack Sullivan put it in 1938, the belief in a unique personal individuality, endemic among psychotherapists and their patients, is "the very mother of illusions."[15]

Buddhist "insight" proposes to clear up this confusion. Although this insight is not the same as psychoanalytic insight, it has not been unanticipated in psychoanalytic circles. Jacques Lacan emphasized the manner in which the developing infant "assumes an image" of himself from the mirror, allowing that image to come to symbolize the "mental permanence of the I."[16] This image becomes established as an ideal that is inevitably compared with actual experience, but it is an illusory image that is unconsciously mistaken for something real. Having seen ourselves in the mirror, we think that is who we have to be.

Other therapists have attempted to weed out the reifications that have crept into psychoanalytic theory, paving the way for an appreciation of the Buddhist attempt to explore the notion of self without such habits of thought.[17] Yet what even these

theorists have lacked is the method, the "mental discipline," of
the Buddha's Eightfold Path that can give a *personal* experience
of, not just a theoretical approach to, this question.

From the Buddhist perspective, all of the psychological
transformations described so far in this chapter are preliminary.
Analytic meditation is not possible without these attainments,
but it should certainly not be confused with them. As the great
Tibetan philosopher Tsong Khapa (1357–1419) taught, these
meditative accomplishments (*samadhi*) do not, by themselves,
successfully address the problem of self. He quoted the *King of
Samadhi Scripture* (attributed to the Buddha and dated to 200
A.D.) to this effect:

> *Those mundane persons who cultivate samadhi*
> *Yet do not rid themselves of the notion of self*
> *Get very agitated when their afflictions return. . . .*
> *Yet if they discern precisely the selflessness of things*
> *And if they meditate on that exact discernment,*
> *That causes the attainment of Nirvana;*
> *No other cause whatever will bring peace.*[18]

When the self is investigated on the path of insight, the
experiences of delight always give way to the experiences of
terror. When the powers of concentration and mindfulness are
directed onto the actual experience of "I," a peculiar thing
starts to happen: what had once seemed very stable suddenly
becomes very unstable. The most basic self-feelings become the
primary focus at this stage of practice, and the closer one looks
at them, the more absurd they start to seem. These self-feelings
are suddenly revealed to be nothing but *images*: the reflection
that had assumed an independent existence in the psyche is
seen for what it always was—a metaphor or mirage. This is a
tricky point, similar to the earlier notion that release from the

Wheel of Life does not mean a journey to another abode, only a reperceiving of what was always present. There is no attainment of a higher self in Buddhist theory; instead, only an exposure of what has always been true but unacknowledged: that self is a fiction.

According to Buddhist psychology, this understanding is liberating in specific, identifiable ways. The difficult emotions such as anger, fear, and selfish desire are all predicated on this misperception of self. When the representational nature of self is fully appreciated, therefore, those emotions lose their source of inspiration. This is the common goal of all forms of Buddhist meditation: to expose the metaphorical nature of self and so to remove the underpinnings of the forces that circle in the center of the Wheel of Life.

In stripping away people's cravings to have to be *something*, the insight practices actually allow meditators to function in the everyday world unencumbered by the need to protect the false sense of "I." When the privacy of the self is fully explored, using the tools of concentration, mindfulness, and insight, neither annihilation (nothingness) nor a permanent isolate can be found. Rather, the meditators have a liberating sense of understanding about just how distorted their perceptions have been.

This is the culmination of a long process of self-investigation. The concentration practices expand and contract the spatial view of self, focusing the meditators on feelings of incompleteness, and, simultaneously, opening them up to infinite space. The mindfulness practices cultivate the ability to surrender into the moment, and they elasticize the sense of self by emphasizing its inherent fluidity. The insight practices explode the last illusions of self-sufficiency by zeroing in on a self that breaks up under objective scrutiny.

Self, it turns out, is a metaphor for a process that we do not understand, a metaphor for that which *knows*. The insight practices reveal that such a metaphor is unnecessary, even disruptive. It is enough, these practices reveal, to open to the ongoing process of knowing without imputing some*one* behind it all. When this possibility emerges, the whole question of attachment to meditative accomplishments or to psychological "growth" is muted. As the ninth-century Chinese Zen recluse and poet Huang Po was fond of pointing out:

> Why this talk of attaining and not attaining? The matter is thus—by thinking of something you create an entity and by thinking of nothing you create another. Let such erroneous thinking perish utterly, and then nothing will remain for you to go seeking![19]

To reach this point requires not the obliteration of ego but the development of mental faculties beyond those that are conventionally accepted as adequate for "normal" functioning. The progress of meditation is one route to such development. Freud lamented in his paper "Analysis Terminable and Interminable" that psychoanalysis by itself was unable to produce an ego strong and versatile enough to accomplish his therapeutic goals.[20] By working directly with the metaphorical experience of self, meditation offers a complementary method of ego development, one that fills in the gap that Freud was left struggling with.

PART III

THERAPY

Psychoanalysis was not so formal then. I paid Miss Freud $7 a month, and we met almost every day. My analysis, which gave me self-awareness, led me not to fear being myself. We didn't use all those pseudoscientific terms then—defense mechanisms and the like—so the process of self-awareness, painful at times, emerged in a liberating atmosphere.   —Erik H. Erikson

One does not err by perceiving, one errs by clinging;
But knowing clinging itself as mind, it frees itself.
                    —Padma Sambhava,
          The Natural Liberation through Naked Vision

REMEMBERING, REPEATING AND
WORKING-THROUGH

IT HAS BEEN CLEAR to me for many years that meditation
and psychotherapy have something important to offer each
other and that many of my contemporaries are in desperate
need of both. At first it seemed as if a linear developmental
model made sense: first therapy, then meditation; first consoli-
dating the self, then letting it go; first ego, then egolessness.
But this view turned out to be naive, the result of a false
dichotomy. Progress in one venue seemed to deepen a person's
ability to make use of the other; refusal to do so seemed to
stymie development in either. Was it possible, I began to wonder, for the two to work hand in hand? Did the two systems
actually embrace common goals but use different methods?

Psychotherapy, it seemed, was poised to address a particular
agony of the Western experience, namely, the longing and pain
of self-estrangement. Without some input from this perspective, it appeared, too many Western meditators were vulnerable to using their practices defensively, to trying in vain to
solve their emotional problems without allowing the participa-
tion of a therapist. Meditation, on the other hand, offered the
promise of actual *relief*, the horizon of the Buddha's Third
Noble Truth. There were too many examples of people who
had gone round and round in therapy for years and years,
dwelling in the content of their individual stories but never
breaking through. The story of the Sufi wise man and fool Nasruddin kept coming to my mind as I contemplated the
attempts of people to find relief from psychotherapy alone:

One night some of Nasruddin's friends came upon him crawl-
ing around on his hands and knees searching for something
beneath a lamppost. When they asked him what he was looking for, he told them that he had lost the key to his house.
They all got down to help him look, but without any success.
Finally, one of them asked Nasruddin where exactly he had
lost the key. Nasruddin replied, "In the house."

"Then why," his friends asked, "are you looking under the
lamppost?"

Nasruddin replied, "Because there's more light here."[1]

Freud unquestionably brought incredible light to the psychology of the unconscious, yet searching for relief through the
methods of psychotherapy alone is the equivalent of Nasruddin
searching in the wrong place for his key. In striving to rid the
mind of neurosis, one could dig forever. Even if this were possible, one would still have to admit what D. W. Winnicott coura-
geously declared: "Absence of psychoneurotic illness may be
health, but it is not life."[2] Meditation aims at something other
than conflict resolution or emotional reparation: it offers not
only the key for us to engage directly with life itself but also the
method of developing the mental faculties so that the kind of
working-through that Freud envisioned could actually occur.

As I continued my work as a psychotherapist, I returned again
and again to Freud's classic work on the practice of psychotherapy, "Remembering, Repeating and Working-Through," for it is
in this paper that he lays out the key ingredients for a successful
therapy. How could Buddhist practice make a difference in this
process? I wondered. What could meditation offer to each of
these three domains to prevent the endless psychotherapy that
came to haunt Freud? After all, his reflections at the end of his
life in "Analysis Terminable and Interminable" are enough to
give any aspiring therapist pause:

As is well known, the analytic situation consists in our allying ourselves with the ego of the person under treatment, in order to subdue portions of his id which are uncontrolled. . . . The ego, if we are to be able to make such a pact with it, must be a normal one. But a normal ego of this sort is, like normality in general, an ideal fiction. The abnormal ego, which is unserviceable for our purposes, is unfortunately no fiction.[3]

It is here that Buddhism has the most to offer to psychotherapy, because there are methods of mental development inherent to Buddhist practice that directly affect what Freud called the "abnormal ego." As those methods are applied, the "ego" undergoes a metamorphosis, and therapy becomes much less daunting.

As the first several generations of Westerners to embrace Buddhist practice have demonstrated, meditation, as developed and practiced in the East, does not easily address all of the psychological turmoil of the Western mind. But psychotherapy—of whatever school—keeps coming up against its own limitations: in Freud's well-known phrase, even the best therapy can only return us to a state of "common unhappiness."[4] What happens when the two worlds collide? Can some kind of integration be forged? What follows are my own experiences, as patient, meditator, and therapist, of how the Buddhist psychology of mind has influenced my work in psychotherapy, and of how meditation can affect the key processes of remembering, repeating, and working through.

CHAPTER 8

REMEMBERING

THE FIRST INGREDIENT of a successful therapy, taught Freud, is the remembering of forgotten aspects of childhood experience. Psychotherapists have experimented with different techniques of accomplishing this remembering, such as free association and the interpretation of dreams, and meditation adds another method to this arsenal. When Westerners begin to meditate, they often remember a longing that dates from early in their lives but that has been unconsciously propelling them ever since. One of the primary purposes of integrating Buddhism and psychotherapy is to help people deal with this discovery effectively.

REMEMBERING THE PAST

Freud described three types of remembering that are possible in psychotherapy, three ways of putting the patient in touch with what needs to be completed from the past. The first method, the cathartic view of therapy, stemmed directly from his early interest in hypnosis and consisted of having the patient directly remember a traumatic event, helped by the hypnotic state to bring out that which had theretofore been repressed and presumably "forgotten," kept alive only in the disguised form of the symptoms. This view presupposed a direct channel into the repressed material such that the patient could recover what had actually happened to so traumatize him. For example, when I was in the fifth grade, a classmate of mine was waterskiing with her brother and witnessed the motorboat she was riding in run over and decapitate him. She became blind (what is today called hysterical blindness), and it was not until she could recover the actual memory of the event that she regained her ability to see.

When there are cases of actual physical or sexual trauma, this kind of remembering is possible, but for those of us without a single etiological event in our past, it is useless to search for such pivotal memories. Freud gave this method up soon after abandoning the hypnotic technique, yet it remains the model for many of those still entering psychotherapy, who hope to recover the single lost memory that will release their repressed emotion and return them to a state of full functioning.

Freud's next technique for remembering consisted of following the patient's free associations in order to discover what the patient was unable to remember consciously by sheer force of will. The technique of free association freed the patient from conscious deliberation and allowed material to come forward, as it does in a dream state, without the usual inhibitions. Rather than reaching directly into the past for a traumatic memory, this modification of technique required that the patient overcome her criticisms of her free associations so as to follow them to their logical conclusions.

The essential point here was that, rather than recovering the repressed memory in one grand cathartic motion, the gaps in memory could be filled in through a process of circumventing the resistances. Free association made this adaptation possible, because the defensive functions of the ego—those that strove to keep the disturbing memories out of consciousness—could, in effect, be tricked into relaxing their grip. Even with this modification, however, Freud was still pursuing a clear memory whose recovery would somehow click things back into place.

In his third modification, Freud moved his focus away from the pursuit of the forgotten past and trained his vision instead on the immediate present. By focusing exclusively on what was actually happening in the therapeutic encounter, Freud found, the very resistances that had masked self-understanding could be evoked and then be described to the patient. In this process, patients often recovered their necessary memories, almost as a by-product of the therapeutic exchange. As Freud described it, the analyst "contents himself with studying whatever is present for the time being on the surface of the patient's mind, and he employs the art of interpretation mainly for the purpose of recognizing the resistances which appear there, and making them conscious to the patient."[1]

There are, of course, memories of a different caliber from those that Freud drew much of his early theory from, memories that are not so much about *something* terrible happening but, in D. W. Winnicott's words, about "nothing happening when something might profitably have happened."[2] These events are more often recorded in the soma, or body, than in the verbal memory, and they can be integrated only by subsequently experiencing and making sense of them. In the paper "Remembering, Repeating and Working-Through," Freud refers to such a "special class of experiences" that were not understood at the time of their occurrence but can only be "subsequently" understood and interpreted.[3] It is this class of memory that increasingly has dominated the thinking of psychotherapists as the problems of low self-esteem, emptiness, and alienation have moved to the forefront of their clinical work.

REMEMBERING THE PRESENT

Buddhism, too, sees remembering—a remembering of the present—as central to psychic stability. As difficult as remembering the forgotten past might be, it is more difficult to align our awareness with our actual present-tense experience. All too often, the Buddha found, we are out of sync with ourselves, lost in thoughts of past or future and unable simply to *be* with our immediate experience. Turning this tendency around by repeatedly bringing the attention back to immediate experience was what catalyzed the most profound psychic change.

The meditative technique that became central to Buddhism was that of mindfulness, in which this continual returning of awareness to the here-and-now was established as a practice in and of itself. Indeed, the classic definition of *mindfulness* emphasizes the capacity for remembering, which is essential for its successful application:

> By its means they remember, or it itself remembers, or it is just mere remembering, thus it is mindfulness. It has the characteristic of not wobbling. Its function is not to forget. It is manifested as guarding, or it is manifested as the state of confronting an objective field. Its proximate cause is strong perception, or its proximate cause is the Foundations of Mindfulness concerned with the body, and so on. It should be regarded, however, as like a pillar because it is firmly founded, or as like a door-keeper because it guards the eye-door, and so on.[4]

In a curious twist, the kind of remembering that Freud came to after abandoning the hypnotic technique and modifying his reliance on free association, what he called "studying whatever is present on the surface of the patient's mind,"[5] is exactly the kind of remembering that the Buddha emphasized all along with his

reliance on mindfulness. Freud saw this remembering as something that could only be done in the hours of psychoanalysis; the
Buddha taught that it could be much more far-reaching, that it
could be done steadily and consistently throughout the day. As
Freud came to see, the pursuit of this strategy sometimes yields
important memories that can be valuable in making sense out of
an individual history. Buddhist teachers have tended to deempha-
size the individual, historical memories that surface, preferring to
aim for a constant application of mindfulness, a consistent
remembering, which they have seen as more valuable than any
single revelation about the past could be. Yet, as any practitioner
of intensive meditation can testify, the steady practice of mindfulness meditation will produce all three of the types of memories
that Freud elucidated.

There is often good reason to pay attention to this psychotherapeutic material, to integrate the memories in a manner
consistent with a good psychotherapy. As the two disciplines
begin to interact more and more, this will prove to be one
important linking point between them. Meditation can indis-
putably frame an area in need of therapeutic attention. As Buddhist teachers become more familiar with psychotherapy, and
as psychotherapists become more familiar with meditation, the
contributions that each can make around these recovered
"memories" will become clearer. Let me offer some examples
from my own experience.

TRAUMA

There are times when the practice of meditation can act in a
manner most reminiscent of Freud's hypnotic technique,
directly releasing memories that would otherwise have

remained repressed. This occurs most frequently around issues of psychic or physical trauma, memories of which are often unleashed through the concentration on breath or body sensations that forms the backbone of beginning meditation practice. Depending on the meditator's ego strength and the therapeutic support available, these released memories can be either destabilizing or incredibly healing. They are often violently disturbing and require significant effort to be integrated.

One day not long ago, for example, a man called me soon after completing his first ten-day intensive meditation retreat. A veteran of six years of psychotherapy who had also made good use of twelve-step recovery groups, this man, a science teacher named Joe, had made peace with his abusive upbringing by a violent and rageful father who had terrorized his wife and four children (of whom Joe was the oldest). Joe had gone on to find a career, a network of friends and associates, and, most recently, an intimate relationship of his own that did not bear any resemblance to his parents' troubled one. He was a mature, self-confident, and capable man. At the retreat, however, for reasons that he could not articulate, he found himself quite fearful of watching his breath. It did not feel like the *neutral* object his teachers described it as; it felt dangerous and made him anxious. He avoided attending to the breath, concentrating instead on simply listening to the sounds that surrounded him for the first three days of the retreat, until he felt composed enough to approach his breathing once again. Developing the qualities of tranquility and peacefulness that come with increasing concentration, Joe then had a particularly blissful sitting (which he described as like visiting a fairy godmother's house in a fairy tale). This was immediately followed by the feeling of an iron band constraining his abdomen, hurting him and restricting his breath.

So intense and unpleasant were these sensations that Joe felt unable to work with them meditatively. Nevertheless, he tried to watch the pain with bare attention, although he found it necessary to walk around, lie down, and stretch out, changing his position constantly. No amount of attention, no change in position, no associated thoughts or feelings, no advice from his teachers seemed to affect the intensity of the sensations, which lasted for the better part of the day. Finally, Joe lay in one position and found himself overcome with sadness. He sobbed and shook for several hours and then had a childhood memory that was new for him. He remembered hiding in the closet from his raging father, filling his mouth with rags to stifle his sobbing out of fear that his father would hear him and become even more angry. Attention to the breath had evoked the memory of choking in the closet, where his efforts had been not to attend to the breath, but to hold it so he would not provoke his father's wrath.

Joe knew from his years of therapy that, as the oldest of four children, he had had to set an example for his siblings and stifle his reactions so as not to set off his father. He knew how threatening his own anger could feel. But, as he said to me, "I knew what had been done to me, but not what I had done to myself." Joe had learned to hold his breath in that moment in the closet, had learned how to bind all of his fear and rage and despair in the muscles of his abdomen. For him, attention to the breath was the key that unlocked his emotional experience. The iron band around his diaphragm was the feeling that resulted from his sobbing and holding his breath, with his diaphragm rising and falling until it cramped. This most basic therapeutic realization of how Joe had closed *himself* down came not out of therapy but out of the meditative state, although his years of therapy obviously helped him see the experience through in a way that many other such traumatized people could not.

While an extreme example, Joe's story illustrates the power

of meditation to focus us in on the places in our bodies where fear has taken hold. The concentrated state of the mind in meditation seems to make these states of contraction particularly visible. They are the internalized remnants of chronic defensive reactions, fossilized within the body out of reach of our usual awareness. Uncovering how we ourselves are creating those body sensations, long after the trauma has passed, removes them as concrete objects (like Joe's iron band) with which we identify or from which we recoil. When there has been a specific trauma, there is often a specific focal point in the body that needs to be experienced. When there has been no such single trauma, the somatic experience is often much more diffuse.

ESTRANGEMENT

In my own case, one of my most recurrent feelings during intensive meditation retreats was what felt like a deep well of longing for what I could only conceptualize as true love. Since these retreats involved weeks of silent and steady mindful awareness of thoughts, feelings, physical actions, sensations, memories, plans, and so on, there was ample time for the superficial chattering of my thinking mind to quiet down and for the development of some of the qualities of calm and clarity that are traditionally associated with the meditative state. Yet, even in the midst of such comparatively spacious states of mind, I would often be aware of what felt like a deeper yearning. My situation was roughly analogous to that which Freud described in his discussion of free association. In following the train of my free associations, as one does to some degree in meditation of this type, I kept encountering this feeling, which a psychoanalyst would probably interpret as an early, preverbal memory.

At one point, after about a week at one of my early retreats, out of this spaciousness of mind came a sudden memory of the bodily sensations I had recurrently had as a child alone in the night. My body began to shake uncontrollably on my meditation cushion for the next twenty minutes or so, an experience that eventually gave way to what can only be described as great peace, light, and love. My meditation teachers seemed nonplussed by my experience, but I took it as a sign of the importance of this particular meditation practice for me. Yet my sense of longing, while temporarily abated, did not disappear. In fact, I spent a good portion of my next several retreats trying to recapture that very experience—a notoriously foolhardy endeavor when it comes to meditation, but one that is very common among Western meditators who begin their practice with an inner sense of emptiness or alienation.

Many years later, when I was actually fortunate enough to marry the woman I loved, I found that even this real and palpable love, which I had longed for and had thought out of my reach, did not take away the depth of my longing. In fact, it seemed to bring it out even more. I began having trouble sleeping, found myself becoming insatiably demanding of my new wife's attention, had difficulty with even the most trivial separations from her, and, when I did sleep, was plagued with nightmares of my teeth crushing against themselves. I had come to personify the predicament of the Hungry Ghosts: just as they are unable to swallow the very food that they need because of the pain that it causes, I was unable to receive the very love that I craved because of the depth of my unfulfilled longing. Needless to say, it was time for (more) psychotherapy.

I could, of course, use my meditative skills to calm myself when pressed, but the strength of my identification with the feelings of unassailable isolation were so strong as to require the more specific attentions of a psychotherapist. Meditation had made me exquisitely aware of my predicament and had helped me recover the early feelings surrounding it, but I was still unable to act in a way that was not completely determined by my past experiences.

The key to my recovery lay, of course, in the recurrent dreams of my teeth crushing against themselves, which I came to understand as a potent expression of "oral rage'—my violent resentment at some kind of early parental unavailability. These dreams eventually gave way to others about not being able to get through to a loved one on a telephone: I would forget the number, the phone would not work, the handle or dial would disintegrate, the person would not answer. These dreams ultimately crystallized in an actual memory of my parents leaving me in charge of my younger sibling when I was five years old while they went next door to see friends, instructing me to call them on an intercom they had set up in case I had any problem. Prematurely separated from my childhood dependence, I was raised to be "responsible"; my unresolved anger was my frustrated aggression at not being able to remedy the relationships with my parents. My sleeping problems and frustrated aggression were not helped, I am sure, by the fact that, in accordance with the customs of the times, I was often laid down to sleep, tired or not, at about six o'clock in the evening so that my tired parents could have a little time to themselves. Once I had this additional insight, I was able to manage the difficult emotions with a bit more grace and humor. The actual love that I was finding in my marriage forced me to grieve the earlier loss of my childhood.

THE BASIC FAULT

In fact, this experience of mine, in one form or another, is a rather typical Western predicament. Both meditation and psychotherapy often reveal memories not so much of a specific traumatic event but of the psychic remnants of absence in one form or another. Dependent as we are on the nuclear family, on the attentions of, at best, two overcommitted parents, and oriented as we are to the development of independence, our culture tends to foster the internalization of whatever absence was initially present. Thus, if the relationship with one or both parents is strained, or if the child is forced to grow up before he or she is ready, there remains in that individual a gnawing sense of emptiness, a flaw that the person perceives as lying within himself or herself, rather than in early personal experiences. This flaw, which has been termed the *basic fault*, is often what one remembers in bodily form in meditation.

By the *basic fault*, I refer to what the English psychoanalyst Michael Balint means when he talks about the psychic remnants of inadequate childhood attention, a trauma so prevalent that it has spawned a chronic spiritual hunger in Western culture:

> The patient says that he feels there is a fault within him, a fault that must be put right. And it is felt to be a fault, not a complex, not a conflict, not a situation. . . . There is a feeling that the cause of this fault is that someone has either failed the patient or defaulted on him; and . . . a great anxiety invariably surrounds this area, usually expressed as a desperate demand that this time the analyst should not—in fact must not—fail him.[6]

The trauma involved here is often one of neglect, rather than abuse. It is experienced as a kind of inner emptiness that is not at all what the Buddhists mean when they use the same word. Yet it is precisely this emptiness that is often first uncovered in meditation and that requires specific psychotherapeutic attention if it is not to tarnish the entire meditative experience. From the Buddhist perspective, the closest parallel lies in the descriptions of the hungry ghost realm. Many Westerners require a combined approach of psychotherapy *and* meditation precisely because the hungry ghost realm is so strongly represented in their psyches. This is a phenomenon that is new to the recorded history of Buddhism: never before have there been so many Hungry Ghosts engaged in Buddhist practice. Their prevalence requires some modifications in technique that are best appropriated from the psychoanalytic tradition.

MOTHERS

In Eastern practices, as demonstrated most clearly in the Tibetan Buddhist tradition, remembering of childhood is done primarily to support and enhance meditation. In the West, these memories tend to disrupt it. This point was driven home to me early in my exploration of Buddhist psychology. In my last year of medical school, I managed to spend three months in India, primarily with various refugee Tibetan communities scattered across northern India. For the first six weeks or so, I was in the small village of Dharamsala, nestled in the Himalayan foothills, home of the palace in exile of His Holiness the Dalai Lama. Because I was there as part of a larger research project, one of my companions, Jeffrey Hopkins, was a Tibetan scholar and translator, and a professor of Tibetan studies at the University of Virginia. This was my first real exposure to the breadth of the intellectual tradition of Tibetan Buddhism; my previous studies had focused on the traditions of Theravada, or Southeast Asian, Buddhism. One of the things that impressed me was the Tibetan effort to cultivate compassion and tranquility of mind through specific exercises that were more like guided meditations or visualizations than anything I had ever been exposed to. The most common such exercise involved imagining all beings as mothers.

Since cyclic existence is beginningless, the argument runs, all beings have, at one time or another, been in every possible relationship to one another. Thus, all beings have been both enemies and friends, and it is only through the impact of greed, hatred, and ignorance that the benevolent relationships have soured. The particular exercise involves recognizing all beings as our mothers—feeling their kindness, developing the desire to repay their kindness, feeling love for them because of their potential for this kindness, and developing the wish that they be freed from suffering and its causes. The psychic root of this practice is the unambivalent love that the Tibetan population is able to summon for their own mothers.

This meditation has always intrigued me. I have had a number of Western psychotherapy patients, for example, with no exposure to this particular exercise, who actually did treat all beings as mothers, and the results, in their personal lives at least, were disastrous. Westerners have a difficult time with this practice: their relationships with their own mothers are much too conflicted. Our child-rearing process, our nuclear family structure, and our desire for autonomy and individuation put a great strain on the parent-child relationship. When the child's temperament runs counter to the parent's or when the parent's ambitions for the child obscure who the child actually is, the family unit easily becomes an alienating or claustrophobic environment in which the child must hide out from the very beings toward whom she is most needy. "The family," chuckled my psychotherapy teacher Isadore From, "is the worst invention of a God that doesn't exist."[7]

I had the chance recently to ask the Tibetan master Sogyal Rinpoche, the author of *The Tibetan Book of Living and Dying* and the teacher of hundreds of Westerners in Europe and America, about this practice of treating all beings as mothers. "Oh, no," he laughed, "not for Westerners. I always tell them like grandmother or grandfather."

EAST IS EAST

The starting point, psychologically, seems to be rather different in the two cultures—a point that is not exactly a revelation. It was Rudyard Kipling who first declared the gulf between East and West unbridgeable. East is East, he argued; we need not try to fathom its depths. Among psychotherapists, even Carl Jung agreed, despite his own personal interests. Eastern practices were too foreign, he felt; Westerners must draw on their own philosophical and spiritual traditions for inspiration.[8]

One reason for this foreignness is that the Eastern self is enmeshed in a web of family, hierarchy, caste, or other group expectations from which the only escape is often spiritual practice. Indeed, the spiritual search in the East can be seen as a kind of culturally sanctioned safety valve for the individual self who can otherwise find no privacy. The Eastern practitioner of meditation is motivated by the same need to "find herself" as is the Western meditator, but the starting points are opposite. As one ancient Buddhist text begins, "This generation is entangled in a tangle."[9] This enmeshment, a common thread running through many generations, gives Easterners a certain strength that meditation traditionally builds on.

The person's capacity for empathic awareness, relaxation of outer ego boundaries, emotional attunement and receptivity, and a sense of belonging is accepted as a given in the East. Meditation, as it has been taught in Eastern cultures, uses this capacity quickly to establish a receptive inner environment for spiritual work.

The starting point in the West rarely is an enmeshed self; more commonly it is an estranged one. The emphasis on individuality and autonomy, the breakdown of the extended and even the nuclear family, the scarcity of "good enough" parenting, and the relentless drive for achievement versus affection in our society leave a person all too often feeling cut off, isolated, alienated, empty, and longing for an intimacy that seems both out of reach and vaguely threatening. At the first cross-cultural meetings of Eastern masters and Western therapists, the Dalai Lama was incredulous at the notion of "low self-esteem" that he kept hearing about. He went around the room asking each Westerner there, "Do you have this? Do you have this?" When they all nodded yes, he just shook his head in disbelief. In Tibet, said Sogyal Rinpoche, a positive sense of self is assumed. It is inculcated early and supported through all of the interdependent relationships that are established by the web of family. If a person cannot maintain this positive feeling about himself, he says, he or she is considered a fool.

In the West, the starting point is different. The Western psyche, it seems, is increasingly vulnerable to feelings of alienation, longing, emptiness, and unworthiness—to emotions that, from the Buddhist viewpoint, characterize the Realm of the Hungry Ghosts. We feel unlovable, and we carry that feeling with us to all of our intimate relationships, along with the hope and expectation that such relationships could somehow erase that preexisting feeling. As children, we sense our parents' inabilities to relate to us, their tendencies to treat us as objects or reflections of themselves, and we personalize their inattention, attributing the lack of connection to our own failings. Children are almost always self-referential in this way: they will explain anything that goes wrong by blaming themselves.

MEDITATION AND THE WESTERN SELF

The different starting points in the two cultures are responsible, I believe, for the different ways that Easterners and Westerners experience meditation. In my experience, it is not true, as Carl Jung believed, that the practices of Buddhism are so foreign as to be unintelligible to the Western mind, but it is true that meditation will bring up different experiences, depending on whether the starting point is an estranged one or an enmeshed one. For those, primarily Westerners, who begin with a history of estrangement, meditation will inevitably yield memories of early unmet longings that survive in the form of the basic fault. For those, primarily from cultures outside of the current Western mode, who begin with a history of enmeshment, meditation is much more likely to bring memories of primitive longings for escape, which will be accompanied by all of the guilt and shame over violating family expectations that Westerners now reserve for issues like excessive dependency. The terror that is emphasized in the traditional psychologies is at least in part a terror of breaking out of or loss of the web of enmeshment, of turning one's back on the obligations of family that so define the non-Western self. The story of the Buddha's life, in fact, in which he leaves his father's palace, his wife and young son, and all of the members of his caste who are dependent on him can be read as a metaphor for the need of the enmeshed self to confront the fear of his ultimate separateness.

In our culture, this separateness is often experienced very early in life. One of the consequences of this more common starting point is that meditation practice now tends to stir up these early feelings, just as Freud found that hypnosis, free association, and the careful attention to what is present "on the surface of the patient's mind" will do. This presents today's meditators with something of a dilemma. They often begin meditation practice only to find that they rather quickly uncover remnants of the basic fault which, like my own longing, do not necessarily go away with further meditation. The low self-esteem that accompanies this longing, stemming from the sense that there is something deficient in the person who longs, often requires special attention of a psychotherapeutic kind, which traditional meditation teachers are not trained to provide. As Freud was to discover, there is commonly a compulsion to act out this unworthiness repeatedly, rather than face it directly. Without the help of a therapist or teacher, the person so afflicted will continue to attempt to jettison the unworthiness by magical means. Meditation is all too vulnerable to this kind of misuse. If the basic fault is not exposed and accepted, the longing to fix it will corrupt the meditative experience.

It is here that I have found the greatest need for a combined approach, tailored to the needs of the hungry ghost, as well as to the human realm. Meditation is often extremely efficient at bringing out the basic fault, but rather silent about dealing with it. This does not mean that meditation *cannot* deal with it, but only that it must be adapted for that specific purpose through an interaction with what works from the psychotherapeutic approach. Buddhism's potential contribution to the mastery of the basic fault does not lie only in the ability of its meditations to *elicit* the psychic remnants of the fault. Buddhist meditation, when properly adapted, can also have a critical impact on the other two components of Freud's therapeutic approach, what he called "repeating and working-through." It holds the key, in fact, to resolving the frustrating inability of psychotherapy to move beyond recognition and reconciliation to the far shore of relief.

CHAPTER 9

REPEATING

W E HAVE SEEN how meditation can be a vehicle for remembering and how this is the first way that its therapeutic potential can be tapped. But Freud quickly discovered that remembering was not sufficient to accomplish his purposes—that mere remembering was not always possible for his patients, nor was it always sufficient to clear them of their symptoms. Many people failed to remember anything of consequence from their early life, he found, no matter what modifications of technique he attempted. The "forces of repression," as Freud called them, were often too great to permit so simple a therapeutic process.

Yet there was another phenomenon that came into play in the therapeutic situation, one that Freud came to call "repeating." Rather than recalling a formative experience, most patients simply reproduced it, with one crucial and defining characteristic: they remained unaware of what they were doing. Thus, a patient whose father was relentlessly critical of her in her youth and who had been able to find no interpersonal satisfaction in her adult life might not know how critical she herself had become, but she might act it out in the relationship with the therapist. By bringing awareness to the criticalness in the relationship, as it was being acted out *but not experienced*, the therapist might help the patient come to terms with the original criticalness that existed in her father.

The interesting thing about the phenomenon of repeating is that the material that is repeated is often just what we resist knowing about ourselves, that with which we are most identified but least aware, that which we are least able to remember consciously. "The patient does not *remember* anything of what he has forgotten and repressed, but *acts* it out," wrote Freud. "He reproduces it not as a memory but as an action; he *repeats* it, without, of course, knowing that he is repeating it."[1]

As Freud developed his technique, he moved from studying whatever was on the surface of the patient's mind to studying whatever was on the surface of the patient's way of relating. This required him to perfect a way of being that did not interfere with the patient's "acting out" but that would allow him to perceive it and interpret it back to the patient. This is the origin of what has come to be called the *analytic attitude* or *analytic neutrality*. It is a way of being, or perhaps a state of mind, that encourages the emergence of the transference, the special relationship between therapist and patient that contains the seeds of whatever the patient resists knowing.

Freud's primary method of wresting away the patient's weapons of resistance was through "analysis" of them. He hoped that if he could interpret to the patient what he or she was unconsciously repeating, the underlying conflicts or traumas could be brought to the surface and respite could be gained. In drawing on both the Freudian and the Buddhist traditions, however, I have found that relief does not often come through verbal analysis alone. As important as it is for the therapist to become aware of what the patient repeats, it is more important that the patient acquaint herself thoroughly with it. Interpreting the repetitions is not enough; the patient must be helped to experience that which she repeats but remains unaware of. It is here that the Buddhist emphasis on fully experiencing each moment dovetails with the Freudian emphasis on attending to what would otherwise be ignored.

The psychotherapeutic environment is a unique domain; it permits the patient to manifest behaviors and feelings that would almost certainly be kept in check or ignored outside of the therapeutic relationship. As such, it presents a tremendous opportunity to put the kind of awareness that the Buddha taught to good use. When the therapist tries not only to interpret the patient's defenses verbally but also to help her *experience* those defenses as *hers*, then the lessons of Buddhist meditation can become therapeutic.

THE HERE-AND-NOW

Freud's discussion of repeating brings up a number of interesting issues vis-à-vis meditation and psychotherapy. With his technique, Freud perfected a method of examining *unaware* repetitions, ones that tend to intrude on and color present-day interactions. The Buddha's technique made the repetitive application of awareness the cornerstone of his successful practice. Freud strove to make his patients less unaware, whereas the Buddha taught his students how to become more aware. Buddhism does not attempt to work explicitly with the unaware repetitions that so fascinated Freud, and yet its method—the repeated application of mindfulness—is congruent with the attentional strategies that Freud found most useful. In developing an approach that draws on both traditions, I have found that each needs something from the other in order to work most effectively.

On the one hand, the therapist's state of mind—his or her ability to work exclusively in the present as the analysis of transference demands—has proved to be a tremendous stumbling block for psychotherapists. Most simply cannot command the kind of attentional presence that Freud found necessary for his work. There is no method for teaching therapists how to attend in this critical way. As a result, most therapists offer, at best, a watered-down version of what Freud was actually able to muster. On the other hand, meditation practitioners and their generally psychologically untrained teachers are often unambiguously unable or unwilling to handle the transference material that will inevitably emerge, as Freud points out, from careful attention to present-day activities and relationships. Meditation, as noted earlier, can bring up lots of emotionally loaded material, which, if not dealt with efficiently, may suffuse the entire meditative experience without ever being effectively put to rest. And yet, when the two traditions are able to work together, they can do so quite harmoniously. By offering the tools of *how* to stay in the present, meditation aids both therapist and patient; by teaching people how to identify and contain past material, therapy can free a meditation of emotional travail. Both work toward a greater ability to face life as it is; both begin, often enough, in silence.

SILENCE

My first experience of transference occurred not in the office of a psychotherapist but in the halls of an Eastern temple in a small northern Indian village called Vrindavan, said to be the birthplace of the Hindu god Krishna. I was attending the festivities at the opening of a new temple dedicated to the memory of a recently deceased holy man who had been the teacher of several of my friends. One of this teacher's chief disciples was a woman named Siddhi-ma, who was sitting on a cot in one of the temple rooms one morning casually giving *darshan*.

Darshan is a phenomenon of Indian religious culture in which devotees of a particular spiritual teacher come to that teacher simply to be with her for an instant. Talking is not a big part of the interaction, yet the experience is often highly esteemed and much sought after. The teacher is said to *give darshan*, or the devotee is said to *receive* it. While little oral communication occurs, the teacher's silence does not convey absence or lack of interest. The teacher is very much present, and her presence, conveyed through the quality of her attention, is a powerful emotional force that evokes a strong response. I am often reminded of this when I sit in my office doing psychotherapy. Freud spoke of psychoanalysis as the "talking cure," and yet what he first cultivated was the therapeutic use of silence. One thing I have learned through my study of meditation is how not to fear this silence. Nowhere in my training as a psychiatrist was this ever emphasized, and yet it has become one of the cornerstones of my work as a therapist. It is not that I endeavor to become a blank screen or a mirror or some caricature of the ever-silent and unresponsive analyst; in fact, I talk quite a bit when I have something to say. But I am not afraid to let there be silence, and I know that my silence does not have to be felt as an absent one.

Let me return to my experience in India: I was encouraged to enter the room, in which about fifteen people were sitting, some on the floor, some on the cot next to Siddhi-ma. I knelt down toward the rear of her chamber. I spoke no Hindi, she spoke no English, there was no one volunteering to act as a translator, and yet when she glanced over at me, I was filled with such a sweet, sad feeling that my eyes began to water. In that moment I felt the wrenching loss of my childhood connection to my own mother. It was a preverbal memory that had been preserved in my body, but one that I had been previously unaware of. It was also the source, I can see in retrospect, of what I was to later repeat in the early days of my marriage.

Siddhi-ma's gaze had evoked this experience, permitting me momentarily to own an element of my personal life that I had been too undeveloped to understand when it had happened. I knew, in that moment, that my own capacity for love had, in fact, not been irrevocably damaged, despite the sadness that I was experiencing. After I had been sitting there a few minutes, Siddhi-ma glanced over at me again, smiled, and motioned to her attendants to give me some *prasad*, milk sweets wrapped in silver foil that had been blessed and were symbolic of spiritual nourishment. They forced me to eat quite a few while they all laughed.

Whether or not Siddhi-ma actually was aware of what had happened to me in that moment or had had anything at all to do with it I do not know. In that very village, in fact, there was an ancient Hindu temple in which darshan was given by a piece of black volcanic rock that was kept behind a curtain at the front of the crumbling temple and that was dressed in a special cloth and attended to by Brahmin priests. The dimly lit temple amphitheater, like an auditorium but without seats, was filled with people round the clock. Several times an hour the curtains would be drawn open for an instant to reveal the black rock to the crowds, who would make all kinds of commotion and have all kinds of emotional experiences upon being in the presence of the rock. The experiences there seemed every bit as powerful as the one that I had undergone.

The lesson for psychotherapy is that the therapist may well have as great an impact through her *presence* as she does through her problem-solving skills. Especially when the root of the patient's emotional predicament lies in the basic fault, in experiences that were preverbal or unremembered and that left traces in the form of absence or emptiness, the therapist's ability to fill the present moment with relaxed attentiveness is crucial. It is not just that such patients tend to be extraordinarily sensitive to any falseness in relating, but that they *need* this kind of attention in order to let themselves feel the gap within themselves. It is much too threatening otherwise.

It is through the therapist's silence, through his or her evocative presence, that this feeling can emerge in the here-and-now. The silence that I am referring to is not a dead silence, not a paralyzed one, but a silence teeming with possibility and texture. In the Buddhist tradition of Southeast Asia, there are twenty-one different words for silence: the silence between thoughts, the silence of a concentrated mind, the silence of awareness, and so on. Psychotherapy requires a silence that permits a patient to act out whatever she is otherwise out of touch with, or to say what she has not previously allowed herself to think. We are all hungry for this kind of silence, for it is what allows us to repossess those qualities from which we are estranged. Meditation practice is like a mine for this healing silence, which is an untouched natural resource for the practice of psychotherapy.

When a therapist can sit with a patient without an agenda, without trying to force an experience, without thinking that she knows what is going to happen or who this person is, then the therapist is infusing the therapy with the lessons of meditation. The patient can feel such a posture. This is most important during the patient's own silences, for when he falls silent, he is often just about ready to enter some new and unexplored territory. The possibility of some real, spontaneous, unscripted communication exists at such a moment; but the patient is, above all, sensing the therapist's mental state to see whether such communication will be safe. A patient can be exquisitely sensitive to the therapist at such times.

It is this mental state, described in another form centuries ago, that makes psychotherapy interesting for the patient: "Do not think, scheme or cognize," counseled an ancient Tibetan meditation master.

> *Do not pay attention or investigate; leave mind in its own sphere . . .*
> *Do not see any fault anywhere,*
> *Do not take anything to heart,*
> *Do not hanker after the signs of progress . . .*
> *Although this may be said to be what is meant by non-attention,*
> *Yet do not fall a prey to laziness;*
> *Be attentive by constantly using inspection.*[2]

It is both tremendously difficult *and* a great relief for the patient to be "held" in this particular state of mind. It is difficult because this experience tends to force up the incomplete or unresolved material in the patient's psyche, her actual reasons for seeking therapy (as opposed to her stated reasons), and it is a relief because this kind of attention, or some derivative of it, is what we are all seeking. When I am asked how Buddhism has influenced me as a therapist, I am often tempted to assert that it has not: that when I do therapy, I am just doing therapy; that being interested in meditation has nothing to do with it. Yet I know that this would be a facile reply. Meditation has allowed me to be a functional therapist: it is through meditation that I have learned how not to interfere at the most critical junctures of the treatment.

W. R. Bion was one psychoanalyst who grasped the therapeutic power of this frame of mind. He also attempted to teach its use to an often confounded and sometimes hostile audience of therapists. Although born in India, Bion did not admit to any influence from his native land. He developed his own idiosyncratic way of describing the therapeutic potential of his state of mind, as indicated in his book *Attention and Interpretation*:

> It is important that the analyst should avoid mental activity, memory and desire, which is as harmful to his mental fitness as some forms of physical activity are to his physical fitness. . . . If the psycho-analyst has not deliberately divested himself of memory and desire, the patient can "feel" this and is dominated by the "feeling" that he is possessed by and contained in the analyst's state of mind, namely, the state represented by the term "desire."[3]

Bion was describing something that Freud had already recognized: the silences between therapist and patient can be either tremendously fertile or terribly destructive. There is a silent communication occurring during such times: the patient is sensing the therapist's mental state, and the therapist can intuit much from the patient. Freud believed that there was a direct communication between the patient's and the analyst's unconscious, in fact, and that it was up to the therapist to foster this environment.

NOT INTERFERING

While Freud aptly described this attentional stance, he emphasized only the value for the therapist in catching the drift of the patient's unconscious. What he did not describe is what Bion hinted at: the impact of this state of mind on the patient. The state that Freud described is necessary because it is only in this state that the therapist's mind will not be felt as an intrusion by the patient. The therapist's expectations and desires, however subtle, create a pressure against which the patient is compelled to react or with which the patient is compelled to comply. The analogy with the intrusive or ignoring parent cannot be exaggerated.

Indeed, the French psychoanalyst Janine Chasseguet-Smirgel has explicitly referred to this capacity for nonverbal communication as a function of the therapist's maternal aptitude. Those who question its usefulness, she insists, must have hidden fears of their own feminine side.[4] It is this fear of the feminine that also makes the meditative state so threatening to many psychotherapists. They refuse to offer the state of mind that, by its very nature of noninterference, allows patients to discover their own sticking points. The Buddhist word *sunyata*, or emptiness, has as its original, etymological meaning "a pregnant void, the hollow of a pregnant womb." When a therapist is able to create such a fertile condition, through the use of her own silence, the patient cannot help but come in contact with that which is still unfinished and with which he is still identified, albeit unawares.

I was reminded of this recently when sitting with a patient who had several years before, after an attack by a mugger, begun to remember sexual encounters with her father. As is common in such cases, this woman was filled with doubt about the truth of her own recollections, but she was gradually allowing herself to consider that they might, in fact, be true. She had had a dream the night before that her purse had been stolen and her wallet, with all of her identification, lost. She told me this at the beginning of the session, before she had really settled down, and she did not look at me much as she recounted the dream. This was not an unusual state for her at this time in her therapy; an affair with an abusive man had ended recently and she often appeared distraught and frightened during these days, like an animal suddenly trapped by a hunter.

A long silence followed her report. Still uncomfortable, my patient also reported feeling suddenly very confused. I urged her not to discount this feeling of confusion but to stay with it, as she was clearly dissatisfied with the feeling and was treating it only as an obstacle to understanding the dream. It was confusion that had emerged out of the void of silence and with which she was still identified; the confusion was the unfinished material that the dream had brought into awareness.

Her next memory was of coming downstairs to the family dinner table after a frightening encounter with her father and seeing him sitting there presiding over the meal. "Now who was she?" she remembered thinking about herself as she looked around at her parents and siblings, all acting so normal. This was the seed of her confusion. Unable to reconcile the two pictures of herself and her father, she had for years denied the truth of what had continued to unfold secretly between them. Her dream, beyond the obvious connotations of rape symbolized by the loss of her purse, brought out the more insidious consequences of that trauma—the confusion that had plagued her and that she had been forced to act out in her repeated involvements with dishonest men, rather than experience consciously.

I was responding meditatively when I permitted my patient's confusion. I did not know what it signified when I urged her to attend to it; I knew only that it could be treated not as an obstacle but as an interesting phenomenon in its own right. My own training in moment-to-moment awareness prepared me for this approach, and my ability to maintain my attentional stance permitted my patient to go more fully into her own experience.

MEMORY AND DESIRE

As explicit as Freud was about the critical importance of evenly suspended attention, therapists ever since have had great difficulty in accepting his advice. "It is too difficult," they complained. "How is it to be done?" they asked. "A strain of this kind scarcely occurs otherwise in life," sighed Sandor Ferenczi.[5] What about intellectual activity, "critical scrutiny," "problem-solving thinking," or "cognitive processing," they asked? Otto Fenichel, who single-handedly codified much of psychoanalytic technique in his still-influential little red book of 1938, *Problems of Psychoanalytic Technique*, dismissed the efforts of those who struggled to implement Freud's original recommendations by accusing them of merely floating in their unconscious and of doing "hardly any work at all."[6]

What all of these analysts failed to understand—and it is hard to blame them, since they had had no experience in meditation—is that a single state of mind, a poised and balanced state of bare, or evenly suspended, attention, can encompass both nonverbal *and* rational or intellectual thought. The cognitive processing does not have to be initiated by the therapist; there is more than enough of it happening of its own accord. When there is something meaningful to say, it is more than apparent. More often than not, however, intellectual activity in the therapist is a defense against experiencing the patient's silence, a refusal to enter the jointly experienced not-knowing that makes discovery a real possibility.

What is ultimately therapeutic for many people is not so much the narrative construction of their past to explain their suffering, but the direct experience, in the therapist's office, of the emotions, emotional thoughts, or physical remnants of emotional thoughts with which they are stuck. These feelings peek out of the silences and manifest their presence when the room becomes quiet. Often in the form of an angry neediness, a sullen hurt, or a hopeless rage, they are the evidence of the basic fault that has people repeating destructive behavior without understanding why. The American Zen teacher Charlotte Joko Beck describes the essence of Zen as learning how to *melt* the *"frozen blockage of the emotion-thought."*[7] Meditation has a dual influence in this regard: it can teach the therapist how to let these most private feelings emerge in the therapeutic communication, *and* it can teach the patient how to be with them once they do. Only then can there be the possibility of bringing the endless repetitions of emotion to a close.

APPLYING BARE ATTENTION IN THERAPY

Once the therapeutic relationship is well enough established to permit the patient to begin repeating the unresolved emotions of the past, the task of therapy shifts to one of learning *how* to be with those very feelings. It is here that meditation, once again, can be specifically of use. Just as the therapist is never really taught how to pay attention in the most effective way, the patient is never taught how to pay attention either. As therapists, we expect our patients to free associate, but we do not teach them how to do it. In particular, when a patient is experiencing a difficult emotion, the method of bare attention can be extremely useful in countering the usual tendencies to act out or hide from the actual feelings. Much of my work as a therapist with a meditative perspective involves teaching people, in the context of therapy, *how* to pay attention to what they are repeating in a manner that is both meditative and therapeutic.

The emotions that we repeat are those we are most identified with and least aware of; they are what we resist knowing in ourselves and what we are in the most need of applying bare attention to. As the well-known behaviorist Marsha M. Linehan described it in a panel that I was a part of in 1988 entitled "The Buddha Meets the West: Integrating Eastern Psychology and Western Psychotherapy,"[8] even the most emotional or suicidal "borderline" patients turn out to be essentially phobic toward their own emotions. They display—or, in Freud's words, repeat—plenty of emotion, but they are simultaneously estranged from and fearful of those very aspects of themselves that are so apparent to everyone else. As Linehan found, the principles of bare attention can be distilled and taught in a behavioral mode with such patients to desensitize them to their own emotions. A similar process is necessary within the parameters of psychotherapy.

This was very apparent in the work I did with a woman named Eden, who, for a long time, gave no indication of making any progress in her therapy. At the age of forty-two, for example, Eden could not be in the same room with her mother for more than twenty minutes without berating her for her failings. Eden was not happy with herself when she acted this way, but she could not help herself; her behavior was the expression of a deeper pain. Resentful over the paucity of interest that her mother had been able to offer her in her youth, Eden would lash out every time her mother made a vaguely disparaging, questioning, or intrusively demanding remark, which was quite often. Thus, when her mother raised such questions as, "Who is staying with the children when you go out?" or "What did you give the kids for supper tonight?" or "Why is the little one upset today?" Eden interpreted those as critical commentary on her own abilities as a mother, which they probably were. Her rage at these questions, however, was of an adolescent nature; she could not muster any of the maturity that she evidenced in other dimensions of her life in her interactions with her mother. Her demand, always frustrated, was to be treated *differently* by her mother. Her need for reparation was so strong that after leaving a holiday dinner at her mother's home one time, she called to confront her mother for not bothering to give her a hug good-bye. Much to her amazement, her mother had actually embraced Eden on her way out: Eden was completely unaware of the gesture.

Of course, Eden had reason for the strength of her feelings. Her memories painted a picture of a mother-daughter relationship that had much closeness but remarkably little warmth. Her anger at her mother's failed gesture suggested some early and ongoing temperamental mismatch, at the very least. Her later memories bore out her mother's difficulties in sensing or responding to Eden's needs. Between the ages of twelve and fifteen, for instance, while Eden's body was changing and developing in adolescence, her mother had ignored these changes and had sent her to school in her childhood clothes. Eden had felt ashamed of her body and had been unable to ask her mother for help, fearing that she would be further ignored. At the same time, her mother was overinvolved in other aspects of Eden's life, since she commented repeatedly on Eden's weight and eating habits, which encouraged Eden to hide from her mother what she was eating. Finally rescued only by a visit to the family doctor, who ordered Eden's mother to clothe her properly, Eden continued to feel ignored and unseen, and as if there was something terribly wrong with her. She once wrote her mother a letter telling her of her pain and her feelings of being invisible, and left the letter on her mother's pillow. Her mother never responded.

As an adult, Eden was drawn to the philosophy of Buddhism, but she resisted formal meditation practice. She couched her resistance in the language of independence: she did not want to submit to some kind of artificial structure, she could meditate her *own* way, and she did not trust some other imperfect teacher to tell her what to do. But Eden came to see in therapy that she was actually afraid of her own pain. Her troubled relationship with her mother had led her to feel so unworthy and so hurt that she could never allow herself to be with those deep feelings about herself. Instead, she kept throwing herself at the original problem in a vain attempt to receive some other message from a mother who must have been feeling equally alienated from her.

In therapy, Eden did not act out her anger, as she did with her mother. For a long time, she simply described the details to me without much emotion. Then, one day, she just cried. This continued for many weeks with neither of us knowing what she was crying about. She would just sit down and, sooner or later, start crying. She did not always seem sad when she cried, but nevertheless she sobbed, with intense shame at what she was doing. Not only was she experiencing the hurt and pain of her unsatisfactory relationship with her mother, it turned out, but, probably more importantly, she was letting herself dissolve in my presence. It was this dissolution, which occurs in love and joy as well as in sorrow, that Eden had been denied. Her mother had simply been too uncomfortable with Eden's emotions to permit them to be expressed, as reflected most dramatically in her failure to respond to Eden's letter. The shame that Eden felt around her emotional expression reflected the shame she had always felt at not being what her mother had wanted her to be. She had been forced to erect her ego boundaries prematurely to deal with her mother's demands and had always felt that it was too dangerous to surrender to her own feelings. Her uncontrolled rage at her mother in her adult years only reinforced that perception of her feelings as dangerous and out of control.

Eden's mother had been concerned about preparing Eden for the outer world; she had never thought to reach out to her daughter's inner world. Therapy allowed Eden to stop expecting anything different from her mother, and to accept the hurt, the pain, and the unworthiness as the natural consequences of the imperfect relationship that she had with her. The work here was in some way the opposite of the Tibetan practice of seeing all beings as mothers. Eden had to stop seeing her mother as *mother*: she had to treat her as just another person, and so tolerate the minor insults that had previously been too redolent of her childhood experiences. My most helpful contribution, however, lay not in any analysis of Eden's predicament, but in my ability to create an environment in which it became safe to experience the forbidden feelings of the past.

REPARATION

While any of the difficult emotions (anger, desire, excitement, shame, or anxiety, for example) may become the focus of this kind of therapeutic bare attention, the constellation that is particularly common involves the striving for reparation that Eden's story is so evocative of. What many of us cannot adequately remember, but instead repeatedly act out, are the consequences of a childhood drama in which, as we have seen, we are left like Oliver Twist, belatedly asking for more. The feelings involved are of being prematurely detached or disconnected, of feeling unreal or forgotten. A common consequence is to feel, as one of my patients described it recently, as if "everybody hates me" or as if one is intolerably alone. Another is to clamor for attention from someone who has proved over and over again to be incapable of providing it.

As Freud found out rather quickly, we rarely are able to remember or experience the traumatic events of our childhood directly, either through meditation *or* psychotherapy. It is much more likely that we will repeat behaviors that are in some way an attempt to repair or deny the original deprivations. As Eden demonstrated in her relationship with her mother, it is much easier to angrily demand complete parental attunement than it is to tolerate the imperfect relationship that actually has always existed. We make these demands for reparation relentlessly, hoping against hope that we can fix our relationship with our parents, achieve the kind of wordless surrender with a loved one that we never experienced, or reach some kind of rapport with those who have disappointed us in which they will no longer be disappointing. The drive in these behaviors, however, is always to change the other person, never oneself.

My work as a psychotherapist is about how we can change ourselves. In cases like these, people must learn first to look at what they are repeating (the rage, the attempts to destroy the separateness that disappoints, the sullen yearnings for attention) and then to feel the inner emptiness that is behind the demands for reparation. It is this emptiness, with which those who are scarred by the basic fault are so identified, that must be held in the attentional space of bare attention. It is often fought against with all of the fury of a rejected lover, but by helping people work their way back through defensive feelings of outrage to the direct experience of that terrifying hollowness, the fear that so permeates their perception of themselves can be slowly divested. This is a goal that psychotherapy has long cherished, but it is one that is made more approachable through the contributions of meditative awareness.

*   *   *

THE GAP

During my earliest days as a therapist, I was taught this lesson about the urge for reparation when a young woman named Paige entered therapy with me after dropping out of college and threatening suicide. She felt empty, without direction or support from her family, and she was afraid of being humiliated in relationships that she both craved and feared. In the beginning, she was tortured by frightening dreams in which she was recurrently chased, threatened, accosted, or pursued. She began calling me often between sessions, sometimes pleading despairingly for help and sometimes expressing indignation and outrage at the ways I was failing her, demanding that I call her back, schedule additional appointments, and drop everything to take care of her. I very quickly began to feel as if I could never do enough, although I tried my best to be helpful, to placate her, to explain the limitations of my role, and so on. All of these attempts at being reasonable did very little to help Paige. It was only when I was able to see that she was, in effect, trying to destroy me, that she did not want to experience the boundaries between us, that her need for me was also mixed with rage, and that she was terrified at the intensity of her fury and needed help with her fear, that I could begin to be a "good enough" therapist.

Paige was repeating, in her relationship with me, much of the fury that she felt over her parents' unavailability to her as a small child. But she was experiencing that fury with me and had no immediate interest in tracing it back to her early life. My first task was to help Paige find a way to experience her feelings without merely acting them out. As angry as Paige was, she was not completely aware of herself. She was possessed of a righteous fury; she felt entitled to make demands on me, and she actually was more in touch with her righteousness than with her rage. Her dreams contained her fury, but always in a turned-around form: people were chasing and threatening *her*, never the other way round. Paige saw her anger as a faucet that could not be turned off, and she was scared to simply be angry, to be with her feelings in a tolerant way. When I forbade her to call me between sessions, when I made clear boundaries that I adhered to, Paige felt a curious kind of relief—and a more circumspect kind of anger at me—that enabled her to begin to focus on the shadowy pursuers of her dreams as her own dissociated angry feelings. Paige was able to take possession of her anger by learning what it meant to *feel* angry, and she became much more human, no longer dwelling in a realm of hideous projections.

Once Paige learned how to be with her own anger, she became much more able to grieve the irrevocable loss of her childhood. Instead of perpetuating conditions in her present life that would reinforce a sense of isolated and alienated bereftness, as she had been doing with me, Paige began to learn how to accept those feelings as a consequence of her childhood experience. By repeatedly applying meditative awareness to those bereft feelings, by slowly desensitizing herself to them, Paige was able to come to terms with who she had become and to reach out toward that which she wished to be.

GHOSTS INTO ANCESTORS

The therapeutic process, then, is one that encourages just this kind of grieving. The psychoanalyst Hans Loewald wrote of transforming the *ghosts* that haunt patients into *ancestors*, through tasting what he called the "blood of recognition" in the relationship with the therapist. He asserted that the ghosts must be led out of the unconscious, reawakened through the intensity of the therapeutic relationship, and then laid to rest, relegated to history, thus allowing the person more flexibility and intensity in present relations.[9] In a similar vein, the British psychoanalyst Michael Balint, in his discussions of the basic fault, wrote of helping the patient change "violent resentment into regret,"[10] helping her to come to terms with the scarring that has been established in her psyche. Implicit in these widely cited analogies is the recognition that the difficult emotions generated by the original deficiencies do not actually go away; they may be enshrined on a shelf above the doorway as in a Confucian home, but they must be afforded great respect.

Once the scarring is identified, once the fault is recognized, once the anger is transformed into grief, the opportunity then exists for meditation to be used in a new way. Precisely because the scarring does not go away, the person then has the opportunity to zero in on the defect around which so much of the feeling of a substantially existent self has coalesced. Westerners who are subject to the basic fault cannot begin to explore Buddhist selflessness without looking first at how they are identified with their emotional pain. This is rarely a process that involves *only* therapy or *only* meditation; it is one that requires as much help as possible. Once cleared of the "violent resentment" that so clouds the observing mind, however, the process of working through can actually begin.

When Freud imagined *how* to make the therapeutic relationship a vehicle for working through these repetitive emotions, he said some interesting things. The emotions must first be given the right to assert themselves "in a definite field," he maintained. The relationship must then become like a "playground" in which "everything that is hidden" can reveal itself. What happens in therapy must be like an "intermediate region" between illness and real life,[11] a kind of twilight zone of the soul.

While many would consider Freud's musings overly idealized, his major omission lay in his failure to teach his followers *how* to create the kind of environment that he imagined. Meditation is indispensable in demonstrating to both therapist and patient how to maintain Freud's "intermediate region" and how to let an emotion or action "assert itself in a definite field." The Buddha's vehicle of bare attention is one means by which Freud's playground can be constructed.

CHAPTER 10

WORKING THROUGH

I REMEMBER ONCE, not so many years ago, sitting in my therapist's office, telling him of an argument that I had had with someone close to me. I can no longer recall the details, but I had done something to get my friend upset with me, and she had become quite angry—unjustifiably and disproportionately, in my view. I was still obviously angry, too, but I remember feeling upset and frustrated as I recounted the events to my therapist.

"All I can do is love her more strongly at those times," I insisted somewhat plaintively, drawing on my years of meditation practice and the sincerity of my deeper feelings in the hope of freeing my mind from the anger that was brewing.

"That will never work," he snapped, and it was like being hit with a Zen master's stick. My therapist would look at me somewhat quizzically at such times, as if amazed at my foolishness. "What's wrong with being angry?" he would often say.

This interaction has stayed with me because, in some way, it crystallizes the difficulties that we face in trying to integrate Buddhist and Western psychological approaches. *Is* there something wrong with being angry? Can we get rid of it? What does it mean to *work it through*? I have to address questions such as these over and over again in my therapy practice, where it has become clear to me that *working through* an emotion such as anger often means something different from merely eliminating it. For, as the Buddhist Wheel of Life has consistently demonstrated, it is the perspective of the sufferer that determines whether a given experience perpetuates suffering or is a vehicle for awakening. To work something through means to change one's view. If we try instead to change the emotion, or the precipitants of the emotion, we may achieve some short-term success; but we remain bound, by the forces of attachment and aversion, to the very feelings that we are struggling to be free of.

As Freud discovered, he could bring out the troubling emotions or behaviors in the field of the therapeutic relationship, but he could not necessarily make them go away. Merely pointing out the patient's repetitions did not bring those repetitions to a halt, nor did interpreting their infantile sources. Something else was necessary, something that the Buddha's strategy of bare attention also aimed at: the gradual *knowing* of the disaffected material as coming from one's own being. As Freud put it: "One must allow the patient time to become more conversant with this resistance with which he has now become acquainted, to *work through* it, to overcome it, by continuing, in defiance of it, the analytic work according to the fundamental rule of analysis."[1]

So working through, even to Freud, was a process of making whole, of repossessing that from which we have become estranged, of accepting that which we would rather deny. It was also a process of making *present* that which was otherwise buried in the past, so that it could, in fact, be experienced as emanating from one's own person. "We must treat [a patient's] illness, not as an event of the past, but as a present-day force,"[2] Freud insisted.

Working something through, it turns out, means first coming to terms with its inescapability. This was the first message that my own therapist was giving me when he asked me what was wrong with being angry. It is also the conclusion that one inevitably arrives at in dealing with what I have described as the basic fault. This "scarring in the mental structure"[3] that takes the form of anger, shame, or bereft aloneness must finally be accepted just as it is, stripped of the futile demands for reparation that otherwise obscure its direct apprehension. This is what Freud was implying when he spoke of treating the illness "as a present-day force." In the practice of bare attention, Buddhism offers the method for widening one's view of troubling emotions and for accepting them as a present-day force. Just as free association, transference, and the analysis of resistance can be expected to bring out the scarring, so bare attention provides the vehicle for making it one's own. This is the therapeutic maneuver that Freud described in "Analysis Terminable and Interminable" as being so difficult to achieve. Working something through, it seems, involves not just the remembering or repetition of repressed material but the acquisition of perceptual skills that permit a development in what the psychoanalysts call the ego. Buddhism has always presented meditation as a form of mental development; psychotherapy has come to a place where it, too, has recognized the need for something more than mere insight. It can turn to Buddhism for instruction in how to accomplish this.

THE IT

When we begin therapy, just as when we begin meditation, our emotions often seem dangerous to us. The clue to this, in a therapeutic encounter, is the description of an emotion as if it were an independent entity. "This incredible anger came up in me," I might have said in describing my own difficulties with my friend who had so upset me. This indicates a very different way of experiencing anger than if I had simply said, "I got angry." As a therapist influenced by Buddhism, I find that I am sensitive to this kind of disclaimed mode of describing emotion because it is such a good indicator of what has not yet been worked through. The very act of verbally acknowledging one's own connection to an emotion propels a confrontation that is often an important step in the therapeutic process. The Buddha holds up a mirror, remember, to those beings of the Hell Realm who are tormented by anger and anxiety. The therapist, in such a situation, must create "an environment in which one can safely and easily be in bits and pieces without the feeling of falling apart."[4]

As psychoanalysts have continually pointed out, it is the tendency of the neurotic character to become estranged from emotional experience, to see thoughts, feelings, or sensations as "it" rather than "I," to deny fundamental aspects of the self-experience. Correctly understood, the Buddhist perspective is that we are nothing but these experiences: to deny their subjective reality is to further empower them as something fixed, powerful, and out-of-control. The person in such a predicament is then cut off from essential aspects of the self-experience. It is a fundamental tenet of Buddhist thought that before emptiness of self can be realized, the self must be experienced *fully, as it appears*. It is the task of therapy, as well as of meditation, to return those split-off elements to a person's awareness—to make the person see that they are not, in fact, split-off *elements* at all, but essential aspects of his or her own being.

Taking my cue from the progress of meditation, I have found that the first task of working through from a Buddhist perspective is to uncover how the spatial metaphor of self is being used defensively to keep key aspects of the person at bay. When emotions such as anger are described in a disclaimed or dissociated way, they are inevitably experienced as things or entities in their own right, over which the person has little, if any, jurisdiction. This creates a situation that is eerily reminiscent of early trends in psychoanalytic thinking, in which the id was seen as the repository of infantile "drives" that were, by their very nature, "immutable," or incapable of maturation or development.[5]

Just as the Buddhist practices counsel concentration as the method for exploring the spatial metaphor, so has concentration turned out to be the key in therapy to reclaiming the dispossessed and reified emotions such as anger. When the attention is trained on the emotion in question—in particular, on the bodily experience of that emotion—it gradually ceases to be experienced as a static and threatening entity and becomes, instead, a *process* that is defined by time as well as by space. The technique of concentration permits the difficult emotion to be experienced as coming from one's own being, and it can then be understood and accepted rather than feared for its brute strength. So in my own example, when I was able to concentrate my awareness on the bodily feelings of being angry, rather than trying to ward off the dreaded "thing" by countering it with "love," I was able to recognize the inescapability of my response. I had been offended and had gotten angry, yet all was not lost. When I admitted it, I could then begin to relax.

While anger is often a likely candidate for this kind of treatment, the feeling of excitement can also be surprisingly threatening. I was reminded of this recently when a young woman with whom I was working began to tell me about a romantic evening with a prospective boyfriend that had made her disappointingly uncomfortable. "I can see the whole scene," Gwen reported to me the day after that evening. "The romantic music, he's coming to sit down next to me. This anxiety starts welling up. It was so strong, I was out of there."

"You say, 'This anxiety was welling up,'" I responded, pointing out the way in which anxiety was being described as an independent entity. "What happens if you say, 'I got anxious?'"

"It's so intense, so overwhelming . . . " Gwen trailed off, unwilling or unable to rephrase her experience.

Gwen was a good example of someone who had not allowed her anxiety, or possibly her excitement, to become part of her self-experience. Phobic toward her own response, Gwen was unable to experience herself as anxious and was thus unable to remain in any intimate encounter whose excitement or threatened loss of ego boundaries provoked the not-to-be tolerated emotion. As it turned out, Gwen thought that "it was wrong" for her to be anxious in a romantic situation such as this and that she should, instead, "be opening like a flower." Her actual response confirmed a view of herself consistent with one she had developed in response to a critical and rejecting mother: that there was something wrong with her. The flaw, in her view, was the anxiety, which she experienced as a dangerous and threatening entity that could overwhelm and embarrass her, rather than as a temporary and contextual self-experience.

If Gwen had scrutinized herself in classical psychoanalysis, she might have remained estranged from her anxiety and excitement, continuing to see them as dissociated and threatening "others" that she could, at best, learn how to control or regulate. Through the process of learning how to bring awareness to her physical experience of anxiety, however, Gwen began to permit a more spontaneous and alive expression of herself, one that could embrace anxiety as well as intimacy, excitement as well as fear. As she learned that her dreaded anxiety would change over time, and that she could be anxious and intimate simultaneously, Gwen began to permit herself a more varied kind of experience.

Just as occurs in the traditional path of meditation, Gwen began to expand her conception of herself from one that relied exclusively on a spatial metaphor of discrete and conflicting "parts" to a more integrated and cohesive view that was organized around a view of herself as ebbing and flowing with resilience and flexibility. This was a major shift in her self-perception, one that came about through the learning of new perceptual skills that allowed her to be with her own excitement rather than turning it into a fearsome force that threatened to overwhelm her. She was able to move from a position of *conflict*, in which the *should* feeling of "opening like a flower" clashed with her actual anxiety, to a position of *ambiguity*, in which she could tolerate being both excited *and* anxious.

INJURED INNOCENCE

In working through, from a Buddhist perspective, the first step, as in meditation, is to learn to be with threatening emotions in a nonjudgmental way. The next step is to find the sense of "I" that is hidden behind the disclaimed actions and emotions when the spatial conception of self predominates. Thus, Gwen needed to find and accept the "I" who was anxious, and I needed to find and accept the "I" who was angry. As one works in this way, the conflicted emotions become less of a threat to a precariously balanced system and more of a reflection of basic human needs that require attention. Thus, anger can be seen as one's inability or unwillingness to use aggression to overcome a frustrating obstacle, while anxiety can be understood as an inability or unwillingness to admit hunger or desire. By tracing the feeling back to the original unfulfilled need, and to the "I" that could not admit to that need, the process of working through is begun. In many cases, once the need or obstacle is identified and the person admits to being involved, the therapeutic work proceeds quite easily.

This process works very well up to a point. When the traumas of childhood are reached, however—and with them, the impossible demands for reparation that are so characteristic of the Realm of the Hungry Ghosts—it appears to have its limits. When the realization occurs that needs from the past were never and can never be met, that obstacles from the past were never and can never be overcome, there is often a sense of profound outrage. As I have made clear in the preceding chapters, it is this kind of realization that tends to characterize the estranged Western experience in psychotherapy. This very outrage is the hallmark of what has come to be called narcissism: the vain expectation and selfish insistence that one's sense of hollowness should somehow be erased. To assume that by merely tuning into the feelings of outrage we will somehow be released from them is, unfortunately, too naive a view. Reclaiming the disaffected emotion does not, in these cases, bring the situation to a resolution, since the only resolution that can be imagined is to retrieve the connection that is already broken.

Meditation practice actually offers a means of temporarily assuaging this hollowness that is not often accessed by contemporary Western therapies: through the development of states of sustained concentration in which ego boundaries dissolve and feelings of delight predominate. Such states, which in the Buddhist cosmology represent the highest and most pleasurable desire realms, represent developed gratifications that reinforce a sense of optimism, hope, and possibility. But another contribution of the Buddhist approach is even more helpful once one has reached the bottom of one's own outrage. It is, in some sense, the secret weapon of Buddhism, the means by which one can shift the perspective from how outraged one feels to *who it is* who feels it, and thereby appreciate what the Buddhist psychologies consider the *relativity* of the narcissistic emotions.

In the Tibetan tradition, according to the Buddhist scholar Robert Thurman, the best time to observe the self clearly is when we are in a state of *injured innocence*, when we have been insulted and think, "How could she do this to me? I don't deserve to be treated that way."[6] It is in this state, he says, that the "hard nut" of the self is best found; and the self cannot be truly understood, from a Buddhist perspective, until it is seen clearly as it appears.

This state of injured innocence is the Buddhist equivalent of the basic fault, but in Buddhism it becomes a tremendous opportunity rather than a place of resignation. From the Buddhist perspective, to reach this state of injured innocence, to hold the feeling of outrage in the balance of meditative awareness, is the entrance to the path of insight. It is just this moment that all of the preliminary practices of meditation have been leading up to, because the path of insight is, above all else, about investigation into the nature of this "I" that feels injured. Until it is felt, it cannot become the object of meditative scrutiny. So in my practice of psychotherapy, I have to somehow celebrate the appearance of this elusive "I," to convey to my patients at the moment of their most poignant indignation the possibilities that are now open to them. In Zen they might call this the gateless gate, the doorway to the path of insight that, upon close examination, is found to be insubstantial.

The power of this approach in dealing with the intractable nature of the reactive emotions that so color the experience of the basic fault cannot be overestimated. While the first step is to integrate the disclaimed emotions and to find and accept the feeling of "I" that has been displaced, the crucial step, from the Buddhist view, is to shift the perspective from the reactive emotions to the feeling of "I" itself. In so doing, one's investment in outrage is gradually withdrawn and replaced by interest in exploring the nature of "I." The Buddhist view of the mutability of the reactive emotions has always rested on this phenomenon. It is not that the emotions necessarily disappear (although some Buddhist schools go so far as to assert that they eventually do), but that the life goes out of them as the feeling of "I" is found to be so much less substantial than was first assumed. The very emotions that, from the perspective of injured innocence, seem so much a matter of life and death seem, from the perspective of a metaphorical self, to be absurd or, at the very least, relative.

EMPTY OF CONTENT

Within the field of psychotherapy and psychoanalysis there has long been a raging debate over whether or not the so-called instinctual emotions are, in fact, capable of transformation. The classical view holds that they are not—that after repression has been lifted or after anger has been owned, they must still be regulated or modulated by the ego. The alternative view holds that once the disaffected material is integrated through the actions of consciousness, there is an actual change in the way those emotions are experienced. When that happens, this latter view insists, these primitive emotions are felt to be "empty of content."[7]

In this view, the ego need not condemn the instinctual emotions once they are made conscious; the very act of making them conscious empties them of their infantile content. The

Buddhist approach posits an all-important intermediate step in bringing this about. Such an emptying is indeed possible, the Buddhists assert, but it comes not just from making emotions conscious but from carefully examining the underlying feeling of identification that accompanies the emotional experience. In making this identification the focus, the Buddhist approach pulls the rug out from under the reactive emotions while opening up a new avenue for their working through. Such an approach derives directly from the logical progression of the meditative path, in which techniques of bare attention, concentration, and mindfulness give way to those of analytical investigation into the nature of the self-experience. By shifting the attention from the emotion to the identification with the emotion, the emotion is experienced in a new way. It is analogous to the experience of trying to see a distant star with the naked eye: by looking away from the star just a bit, one actually sees it more clearly.

This is an approach that I imagine Freud would have admired. In his writings on the "instincts," he appeared to have developed a similar faith in the power of consistent objective scrutiny to bring about a transformation in consciousness. In so doing, Freud came to conclusions about the instincts that are very close to the Buddha's conclusions about the self. "The theory of the instincts is so to speak our mythology," said Freud in his *New Introductory Lectures*.[8] "Instincts are mythical entities, magnificent in their indefiniteness. In our work we cannot for a moment disregard them, yet we are never sure that we are seeing them clearly."

Psychotherapists using a Buddhist approach would agree, but they would insist on shifting the focus of observation from the instincts to the self, for when the magnificent indefiniteness of the self is realized, the "instincts" become much less significant. This transformation is made possible through the examination of the self that feels injured, not just through examination of the feelings of injury. When the mythical nature of that appearing self is realized, the emptiness of the egoistic emotions can hardly be avoided.

In a psychotherapeutic context this approach is particularly useful because it permits a simultaneous appreciation of the intensity of the reactive emotions *and* of the precarious ground on which they are perched. Working through means coming to terms with both. Consider what happened to my patient Carl, a forty-year-old advertising executive who had an experience on a meditation retreat that crystallizes this discussion concretely.

Carl could take care of anyone. In his therapy with me, he was a masterful storyteller, threading one vignette seamlessly into another so that I was never bored. It took me quite a while to realize that Carl was effortlessly repeating a behavior with me that he had also used in other critical relationships in his life. His stories were so enjoyable and seemingly relevant that he gave the appearance of being deeply involved in therapy, but it turned out that he was deeply involved in taking care of me.

Carl's need to take care of those with whom he was intimately involved and his underlying fear of dependency stemmed most directly from the tragic death of his older brother in an automobile accident when Carl was four. Carl's parents reacted with understandable grief, but their mourning never ceased, nor was it ever discussed. Carl had no memories of his own loss: he became an outwardly cheerful, high-achieving student and athlete who successfully buried his feelings of isolation until the breakup of his first long relationship. Carl's progress in therapy need not be detailed here, but he was able to reach the point that I would characterize as an appreciation of the basic fault. He was no longer hiding from the devastating emotional consequences of his brother's untimely death.

When Carl began to meditate intensively, his experience was

one of relentless and oppressive physical pain. This was not the kind of pain that more frequently characterizes beginning meditation: pain in the back, the knees, or the neck that intensifies but then fades away once the places of muscular tension are experienced and relaxed. This appeared to be a different order of pain, of a quality that soon convinced Carl that he had something physically wrong with him. The pain began preoccupying Carl's attention so fully that he imagined all kinds of desperate scenarios and became panicky. He did everything he could think of to escape from the pain, but that only seemed to make it worse. He felt caught in a vise.

It was not until he had the thought "This is the pain that will *never* go away" that Carl tied his physical experience in meditation to his emotional one in therapy. At this point Carl was able to work with the pain as, in fact, the pain that *would* never go away, stemming as it did from the simultaneous loss of his brother *and* of his parents' affection. Using bare attention, Carl was able to sit with his pain without panicking, but until he was able to shift his focus from the pain to the "I" that was feeling hurt, there was little sense of progress. This shift occurred as Carl found himself repeating the words "I'm sorry, I'm sorry" to himself, as if he had been the person responsible for his parents' grief and emotional unavailability.

Holding this feeling and surrounding it with meditative awareness, Carl began to experience his persistent physical pain as ribbons of light and sensation fluttering up and down his back. His experience was similar to what patients with chronic pain report when they are given effective analgesia: "My pain is the same but it doesn't hurt anymore." Carl knew his pain, his anger, and his guilt thoroughly after this experience, and yet he no longer felt restricted by them. His feelings did not go away, but his compulsive need to be a caretaker did. He was able to have a different kind of intimate interpersonal experience thereafter. This is what it means to empty the instincts: Carl's feelings did not really change, but he was no longer driven by their content.

REDIRECTING AGGRESSION

The power of the Buddhist approach is that, at the critical moment of injured innocence, it deftly redirects one's attention *and aggression* from the disappointing "object" to the misperceived subject. The insistence on reparation is really a barely disguised form of aggression toward the disappointing loved one, a hidden fear that the loss of connection was really caused by one's own hatred or need. By shifting the perspective back onto the felt sense of "I," the Buddhist method permits a full exploration of the vagaries of these emotions, while continually questioning the implicit identification with them that otherwise prevents a thorough investigation. Thus, when I began to take interest in the feeling of self that came with my anger, I had the sense of expanding the field in which that anger was expressed. I felt less guilty, but not any more angry; in fact, I became much more able to treat being angry as an inevitable and fleeting response to a perceived disappointment, rather than as a menacing threat to an inherently unstable connection.

An emotion such as anger can be said to be worked through when its arising permits one to focus on the concomitant sense of "I," when *that* becomes more compelling than the sense of indignation. This redirection or expansion of attention is not developed defensively, so as not to have to experience the anger, but is developed out of the intent to use every opportunity to explore the nature of self. By challenging the agency of an emotion, one can move from a self-referential perspective to a position of openness. While not denying the immediate reality of the feeling, one can nevertheless begin to smile at oneself and at one's habitual reactions.

One of my major discoveries in therapy was that I am made angry by the least interruption of intimate connection. Although I came to understand that this stemmed from a premature feeling of estrangement in my childhood, this knowledge alone gave me insight, but not relief. I remained hostage to my feelings each time a friend or loved one disappointed me. When I became able to use those disappointments to bring my own primitive sense of identification into focus, however, something began to shift. I found that I could not possibly remain so righteously indignant time and again. I was forced to relax my grip and question my conviction that an individual episode of withdrawal needed to be interpreted as abandonment. By tapping my own aggression and using it to redirect my awareness, I prevented myself from being held prisoner by my own instinctive reactions. The ability to make this transition from identification with the thinker to doubt over its reality is what permits an adequate working through of therapeutic discoveries.

As long as the thinker is implicitly accepted, there will always be some narcissistic attachment to the injury that is uncovered in therapy. When that injury can instead be used to pinpoint the elusive sense of self, then it begins to serve some function and can, in turn, be used for a greater purpose. Therapy all too often leaves people in possession of their pain, but without the tools to put it to any use. It can uncover the latent sense of "I," the seed of narcissism, without knowing how to make that discovery worthwhile. Despite therapy, one continues to feel stuck—without a sense of hope or possibility. It was in such cases that Freud despaired of ever being able to terminate analysis.

TERMINATION

The ending of a psychotherapy is the last chance to encourage this shift from injured innocence to investigation of the "I." It represents the final opportunity to use the therapeutic relationship in teaching one how to redeploy awareness away from feelings of injury and toward the emptiness and egolessness that the Buddha taught as an antidote to mental suffering. While this can sound lofty in the abstract, it can sometimes be the most practical method available for helping a person deal with the resurrection of difficult feelings at such a time, because termination always brings out the residual emotions that have not been worked through.

For example, one of my first long-term patients was a man named Jerry, who had often expressed fears about ending his relationship with me. After working together for many years, however, we eventually began to reduce the frequency of his sessions. After a tumultuous therapy, punctuated by episodes in which he would wait outside my office door to jealously time my sessions with other patients, Jerry found himself ready to begin the process of termination. When the time of the first missed session came around, however, Jerry felt as if I was kicking him out. He became angry and hurt and he felt rejected, abandoned, inadequate, and enraged—reactions we had explored thoroughly in his therapy. Jerry could not help reacting this way, even though, from a distant island of clarity, he could recognize the way in which these beliefs did not ring true. This recognition gave him the strength to work with his feelings in the way I have described. By expanding his awareness, as he had learned, to include his own physically felt identification with his feelings of injury, they began to seem absurd to him. The more he focused on the subjective sense of "I," the more able he became to confront the one feeling that he was *not* experiencing: sadness over leaving me. As a consequence, Jerry had the experience not just of being angry with me but of missing me during the week of his missed session. As a result of all of our work together, he was able to accomplish most of this process on his own; my only contribution was to point out how he seemed to be rushing toward the completion of his therapy without stopping to experience what it was like.

WORKING TOWARD

As Jerry became able to miss me, he became much more able to seek out new experiences that had the potential to make him happy. Rather than dwelling in his anger or even in his sadness, he took on the responsibility of finding new ways to keep himself interested in his life. He was able to move from a focus on working through his difficult feelings to one on "working toward"⁹ greater satisfactions. He was aided in this by the Buddhist technique of redirecting attention at the crucial moment of injured innocence, for he was by no means immune to the resentments that he had entered therapy with. He was still prone to exaggerating any perceived slight, but he was able to turn those catastrophic events into opportunities for breakthrough. If the Buddha's promise can be believed (remember that he was reluctant to proclaim it, out of the conviction that it would not be), then the possibility of a greater satisfaction lies ahead for those who are willing to work with their psychic pain in this fashion.

By uncovering not just the unresolvable feelings of narcissistic injury but also the subjective sense of "the injured," psychotherapy can mesh with Buddhism in a way that enhances both. By bringing out the subjective sense of "I" in a sensitive and supportive environment, psychotherapy can do what meditation practice alone often fails to accomplish: overcome the obstacles of a Western mind to find and hold the estranged and alienated self-feeling. By refusing to be put off by the sense of injured innocence that often precipitates out of a successful psychotherapeutic relationship, but instead using that feeling as a springboard for the investigation of the appearing "I," Buddhism offers the crucial link between working through and working toward that has long eluded psychotherapists. This link represents a shift in perspective that can suddenly make a closed situation seem open once again.

This shift, which Buddhism is continually trying to encourage and to describe in new ways, is the most important contribution that Buddhism has to offer to the world of psychotherapy. Just when it seems that nothing more can be done, the Buddha promised that another door can be opened. The Buddha continually used examples of death and loss in his teachings, not because of a belief that it was wrong to have an emotional response to their occurrence (as has sometimes been assumed by eager followers or skeptical critics), but because even these most devastating experiences can be worked with in the way I am describing. We cannot approach a release from emotional pain without first confronting the thinker.

*   *   *

THE ENGINE OF SUBLIMATION

The Dalai Lama begins every talk by describing how human beings yearn for happiness and how the only point of spiritual practice is to make that happiness a reality. The strategy of focusing the attention on the appearing "I" at the moments of narcissistic injury is but an advanced example of an approach that the Buddhist path makes extensive use of: that of consistently working toward more mature satisfactions. The antidote to the heedless desire of the Animal Realm, for example, is portrayed in the Wheel of Life by a book, and the antidote to the bottomless thirst of the Realm of the Hungry Ghosts is described as spiritual nourishment, both of which are potent symbols of sublimation. The ability to *hold* an emotion in the transitional space of bare attention is always portrayed in Buddhist teachings as more satisfying and more complete than the strategies of disavowal or indulgence.

The pleasurable feeling states of the concentration practices are known for their delightful and gratifying feeling tones, and the possibility of becoming attached to their sensual dimension is a sure sign of their being sublimated states of desire. The balanced state of equanimity, like a fine tea, is always praised in the Buddhist literature for the superior pleasure that it affords. Clearly, the Buddhist view is that awareness itself is the engine of sublimation; its cultivation permits the meditator a method of uncovering gratifications that would not otherwise be available. It is in this context that the strategy of penetrating narcissism emerges as the antidote to the scarring of the basic fault, and it was in this context that the psychoanalyst Erich Fromm wrote in his landmark *Zen Buddhism and Psychoanalysis*, "For those who suffer from alienation, cure does not consist in the *absence of illness*, but in the *presence of well-being*."[10]

Yet Fromm was mistaken in equating the Buddhist approach solely with the generation of well-being. As we have seen, Buddhist meditation produces experiences of delight *and* of terror, of sublimated states of desire *and* of aggression. In highlighting only the states of delight, Fromm was making the same mistake that Freud did when he equated the mystical experience with the oceanic feeling. For, as the Buddha taught, states of well-being are inherently unstable; they may temporarily counter the symptoms of alienation, but they are not a cure. Alienation requires meaning, not well-being, in order to be effectively put to rest: what the Buddha offered was a path, a sense of *purpose*, whose generation requires the aggressive reorientation of awareness to include the assumption of identity. At precisely those moments when we are feeling most besieged, when our innate aggression and self-protective feelings are being instinctively evoked, we have the opportunity to work toward greater understanding. The aggression of injured innocence can be harnessed to explode narcissism: this is what is meant by the "destructive potential" of meditation.

When Freud wrote about the oceanic feeling as the apotheosis of the mystical feeling and when Fromm extolled well-being as the fruition of Buddhist meditation, they were overlooking a simple but essential point: meditation is not just about creating states of well-being; it is about destroying the belief in an inherently existent self. "Thoughts exist without a thinker," taught the psychoanalyst W. R. Bion. Insight arises best, he said, when the "thinker's" existence is no longer necessary. This is precisely what the Buddha had discovered many years before. The meditative experience does not have to be oceanic, it turns out, to reveal how much at sea we really are.

Notes

INTRODUCTION: KNOCKING ON BUDDHA'S DOOR

1. Rick Fields, *How the Swans Came to the Lake: A Narrative History of Buddhism in America* (Boulder, Colo.: Shambhala, 1981), p. 135.
2. See the letter of January 19, 1930, from Freud to Romain Rolland in *Letters of Sigmund Freud*, ed. Ernst Freud (New York: Basic Books, 1960), pp. 392–93.
3. Sigmund Freud, *Civilization and Its Discontents*, vol. 21 of *Standard Edition of the Complete Psychological Works of Sigmund Freud*, ed. and trans. James Strachey (London: Hogarth Press and Institute of Psychoanalysis, 1961), p. 72.
4. Sigmund Freud, "Analysis Terminable and Interminable," *Standard Edition,* 23:235. As I discuss at the beginning of part III, Freud came to the conclusion that only a "healthy" ego could fully benefit from psychoanalysis.

CHAPTER 1. THE WHEEL OF LIFE: A BUDDHIST MODEL OF THE NEUROTIC MIND

1. Sigmund Freud, "Remembering, Repeating and Working-Through," in vol. 12 of *Standard Edition of the Complete Psychological Works of Sigmund Freud*, ed. and trans. James Strachey (London: Hogarth Press and Institute of Psychoanalysis, 1958), p. 152.
2. Freud, "The Dynamics of Transference," *Standard Edition*, 12:108.

3. D. W. Winnicott, *Playing and Reality* (London and New York: Routledge, 1971).

4. Freud, "On the Universal Tendency to Debasement in the Sphere of Love," *Standard Edition*, 11:188–89.

5. Freud, *Civilization and Its Discontents, Standard Edition*, 21:76.

6. Michael Eigen, "The Area of Faith in Winnicott, Lacan and Bion," *International Journal of Psycho-Analysis* 62 (1981): 422.

7. D. W. Winnicott, "Communicating and Not Communicating Leading to a Study of Certain Opposites," in *The Maturational Processes and the Facilitating Environment* (New York: International Universities Press, 1965), p. 187.

8. Ibid., p. 186.

9. See Lewis Aron, "Working through the Past—Working toward the Future," *Contemporary Psychoanalysis* 21 (1991): 87–88.

10. See Peter Matthiessen, *Nine-Headed Dragon River: Zen Journal 1969–1982* (Boston: Shambhala, 1987), p. 192.

11. W. R. Bion, *Attention and Interpretation* (New York: Basic Books, 1970), p. 105.

CHAPTER 2. HUMILIATION:
THE BUDDHA'S FIRST TRUTH

1. Narada Maha Thera, *The Buddha and His Teachings* (Colombo, Sri Lanka: Vajirarama, 1973), p. 62.

2. Compiled from ibid., pp. 89–90; and Nyanatiloka, *The Word of the Buddha*, 14th ed. (Kandy, Sri Lanka: Buddhist Publication Society, 1968).

3. Lucien Stryck, *World of the Buddha* (New York: Grove Weidenfeld, 1968), pp. 52–53.

4. Sigmund Freud, *Beyond the Pleasure Principle*, vol. 18 of *Standard Edition of the Complete Psychological Works of Sigmund Freud*, ed. and trans. James Strachey (London: Hogarth Press and Institute of Psychoanalysis, 1955), pp. 20–21.

5. Janine Chasseguet-Smirgel and Bela Grunberger, *Freud or Reich? Psychoanalysis and Illusion* (New Haven, Conn.: Yale University Press, 1986), p. 130.

6. Wilhelm Reich, *Character Analysis*, 3d ed. (New York: Orgone

Institute Press, 1949), p. 213.

7. Otto Rank, "The Genesis of the Object Relation," in *The Psycho-analytic Vocation: Rank, Winnicott, and the Legacy of Freud*, ed. Peter Rudnytsky (New Haven, Conn.: Yale University Press, 1991), p. 173.

8. Otto Rank, *Will Therapy*, trans. J. Taft. (1929–1931; reprint, New York: Norton, 1978), p. 124.

9. Adam Phillips, *Winnicott* (Cambridge, Mass.: Harvard University Press, 1988), p. 81.

10. Ibid., p. 134.

11. D. W. Winnicott, "Ego Distortion in Terms of True and False Self," in *The Maturational Processes and the Facilitating Environment* (New York: International Universities Press, 1965), p. 145.

12. Freud, "On Narcissism: An Introduction," *Standard Edition*, 14:116.

13. Richard De Martino, "The Human Situation and Zen Buddhism," in *Zen Buddhism and Psychoanalysis*, ed. Erich Fromm, D. T. Suzuki, and Richard De Martino (New York: Harper & Row, 1960), p. 146.

14. Stephen Batchelor, *The Faith to Doubt: Glimpses of Buddhist Uncertainty* (Berkeley, Calif.: Parallax Press, 1990), p. 83.

CHAPTER 3. THIRST:
THE BUDDHA'S SECOND TRUTH

1. Sigmund Freud, "Formulations on the Two Principles of Mental Functioning," in vol 12. of *Standard Edition of the Complete Psychological Works of Sigmund Freud*, ed. and trans. James Strachey (London: Hogarth Press and Institute of Psychoanalysis, 1958), p. 219.

2. See T. R. V. Murti, *The Central Philosophy of Buddhism: A Study of the Madhyamika System* (London: Unwin Hyman, 1955), p. 3.

3. From Sutta 63 of the Majjhima-nikaya. Cited in Lucien Stryck, *World of the Buddha* (New York: Grove Weidenfeld, 1968), p. 147.

4. Ananda K. Coomaraswamy and I. B. Horner, *The Living Thoughts of Gotama the Buddha* (London: Cassell, 1948), p. 149.

5. Alice Miller, *The Drama of the Gifted Child: The Search for the True Self*, trans. Ruth Ward (New York: Basic Books, 1994), p. 39.

6. Adam Phillips, *On Kissing, Tickling, and Being Bored* (Cambridge, Mass.: Harvard University Press, 1993), p. 76.

7. Daisetz Teitaro Suzuki, trans., *The Lankavatara Sutra: A Mahayana Text* (Boulder, Colo.: Prajna Press, 1978), p. 159.

8. D. W. Winnicott, "Ego Distortion in Terms of True and False Self," in *The Maturational Processes and the Facilitating Environment* (New York: International Universities Press, 1965), p. 148.

9. Christopher Bollas, *Forces of Destiny: Psychoanalysis and Human Idiom* (London: Free Association Books, 1989), p. 21.

10. Hans Waldenfels, *Absolute Nothingness: Foundations for a Buddhist-Christian Dialogue*, trans. J. W. Heisig (New York: Paulist Press, 1976), p. 68.

CHAPTER 4. RELEASE:
THE BUDDHA'S THIRD TRUTH

1. Joseph Goldstein and Jack Kornfield, *Seeking the Heart of Wisdom: The Path of Insight Meditation* (Boston: Shambhala, 1987), p. 83.

2. Nyanatiloka, trans., *The Word of the Buddha* (Kandy, Sri Lanka: Buddhist Publication Society, 1971), p. 38.

3. Sigmund Freud, "Five Lectures on Psycho-Analysis," in vol. 11 of *Standard Edition of the Complete Psychological Works of Sigmund Freud*, ed. and trans. James Strachey (London: Hogarth Press and Institute of Psychoanalysis, 1957), pp. 53–54.

4. Freud, *Leonardo da Vinci and a Memory of His Childhood, Standard Edition*, 11:74–75.

5. This vignette has also been recorded in Stephen Levine, *Who Dies?* (New York: Doubleday/Anchor Books, 1982), pp. 98–99.

6. Freud, *Civilization and Its Discontents, Standard Edition*, 21:68.

7. Hans Loewald, *Sublimation: Inquiries into Theoretical Psychoanalysis* (New Haven, Conn.: Yale University Press, 1988), p. 13.

8. Lucien Stryk, *World of the Buddha* (New York: Grove Weidenfeld, 1968), p. 271.

9. See, for example, Roy Schafer, *A New Language for Psychoanalysis*

(New Haven, Conn.: Yale University Press, 1976), pp. 155–78.

10. Janine Chasseguet-Smirgel, *The Ego Ideal: A Psychoanalytic Essay on the Malady of the Ideal*, trans. Paul Barrows (New York: Norton, 1985), p. 56.

11. Richard B. Clarke, trans., *Verses on the Faith Mind* (Fredonia, N.Y.: White Pine Press, 1984), p. 155.

12. Philip Yampolsky, trans., *The Platform Sutra of the Sixth Patriarch* (New York: Columbia University Press, 1967), p. 193.

CHAPTER 5. NOWHERE STANDING: THE BUDDHA'S FOURTH TRUTH

1. Thomas Merton, *Mystics and Zen Masters* (New York: Dell, 1961), pp. 18–19.

2. Walpola Rahula, *What the Buddha Taught* (New York: Grove Press, 1974), p. 45.

3. Annie Reich, "Narcissistic Object Choice in Women," *Journal of the American Psychoanalytic Association* 1 (1953): 22–44.

4. His Holiness Tenzin Gyatso, *Kindness, Clarity, and Insight*, trans. and ed. Jeffrey Hopkins (Ithaca, N.Y.: Snow Lion, 1984), p. 40.

5. Robert A. F. Thurman, *Tsong Khapa's Speech of Gold in the Essence of True Eloquence: Reason and Enlightenment in the Central Philosophy of Tibet* (Princeton, N.J.: Princeton University Press, 1984), p. 68.

6. Herbert V. Guenther, *Philosophy and Psychology in the Abhidharma* (Berkeley, Calif.: Shambhala, 1974), p. 207.

7. Kalu Rinpoche, *The Dharma That Illuminates All Beings Impartially Like the Light of the Sun and the Moon* (Albany: State University of New York Press, 1986), p. 111.

8. Richard B. Clarke, trans., *Verses on the Faith Mind* (Fredonia, N.Y.: White Pine Press, 1984), pp. 148–51.

PART II. MEDITATION

1. Ananda K. Coomaraswamy and I. B. Horner, *The Living Thoughts*

of the Gotama Buddha (London: Cassell, 1948), pp. 184–85.

2. Nyanaponika Thera, *The Vision of Dhamma: Buddhist Writings of Nyanaponika Thera*, ed. Bhikkhu Bodhi (York Beach, Maine: Samuel Weiser, 1986), p. 33.

3. Sigmund Freud, *Civilization and Its Discontents*, vol. 21 of *Standard Edition of the Complete Psychological Works of Sigmund Freud*, ed. and trans. James Strachey (London: Hogarth Press and Institute of Psychoanalysis, 1966), pp. 72–73.

CHAPTER 6. BARE ATTENTION

1. Nyanaponika Thera, *The Heart of Buddhist Meditation* (New York: Samuel Weiser, 1962), p. 30.

2. Joseph Goldstein, *The Experience of Insight: A Natural Unfolding* (Santa Cruz, Calif.: Unity Press, 1976), p. 20.

3. See, for example, my articles on the subject: "On the Neglect of Evenly Suspended Attention," *Journal of Transpersonal Psychology* 16 (1984): 193–205 and "Attention in Analysis," *Psychoanalysis and Contemporary Thought* 11 (1988): 171–89. See also Sigmund Freud, "Recommendations to Physicians Practicing Psycho-Analysis," in vol. 12 of *Standard Edition of the Complete Psychological Works of Sigmund Freud*, ed. and trans. James Strachey (London: Hogarth Press and Institute of Psychoanalysis, 1958), pp. 111–12; and Freud, "Two Encyclopedia Articles," *Standard Edition*, 18:235–62.

4. Sigmund Freud, "Analysis of a Phobia in a Five-Year-Old Boy," *Standard Edition*, 10:23.

5. Freud, "Recommendations to Physicians Practicing Psycho-Analysis," *Standard Edition*, 12:111–12.

6. D. W. Winnicott, "The Capacity to Be Alone," in *The Maturational Processes and the Facilitating Environment* (New York: International Universities Press, 1965), pp. 29–37.

7. Wes Nisker, "John Cage and the Music of Sound," *Inquiring Mind* 3, no. 2 (1986): 4.

8. D. W. Winnicott, "Birth Memories, Birth Trauma, and Anxiety," in *Collected Papers: Through Paediatrics to Psycho-Analysis* (New York: Basic Books, 1958), pp. 183–84.

9. Michael Eigen, "Stones in a Stream," *Psychoanalytic Review* (in press).

10. D. W. Winnicott, "Transitional Objects and Transitional Phenomena," in *Playing and Reality* (London: Routledge, 1971), p. 14.

11. Shunryu Suzuki, *Zen Mind, Beginner's Mind* (New York: Weatherhill, 1970), pp. 36–37.

CHAPTER 7. THE PSYCHODYNAMICS OF MEDITATION

1. Bhadantacariya Buddhaghosa, *Visuddhimagga* (Path of purification), trans. Bhikkhu Nyanamoli, vol. 1 (Berkeley, Calif.: Shambhala, 1976), pp. 149–50.

2. Bhadantacariya Buddhaghosa, *Visuddhimagga* (Path of purification), trans. Bhikkhu Nyanamoli, vol. 2 (Berkeley, Calif.: Shambhala, 1976), p. 753.

3. Daniel Brown and Jack Engler, "The States of Mindfulness Meditation: A Validation Study," in *Transformations of Consciousness: Conventional and Contemplative Perspectives on Development*, ed. Ken Wilber, Jack Engler, and Daniel Brown (Boston: New Science Library, 1986), p. 189.

4. Stephen A. Mitchell, *Hope and Dread in Psychoanalysis* (New York: Basic Books, 1993), p. 101.

5. Daniel Goleman, *The Meditative Mind: The Varieties of Meditative Experience* (Los Angeles: Tarcher, 1988).

6. Jack Kornfield, *A Path with Heart: A Guide through the Perils and Promises of Spiritual Life* (New York: Bantam, 1993), pp. 108–10.

7. Nyanaponika Thera, *The Heart of Buddhist Meditation* (New York: Samuel Weiser, 1962), pp. 144–45.

8. Mitchell, *Hope and Dread*, p. 149.

9. Marion Milner, *The Suppressed Madness of Sane Men: Forty-four Years of Exploring Psychoanalysis* (London: Tavistock, 1987), pp. 260–61.

10. Michael Eigen, "Breathing and Identity," in *The Electrified Tightrope*, ed. Adam Phillips (Northvale, N.J.: Jason Aronson, 1993), p. 46.

11. Joseph Goldstein, personal communication to the author, February 1994.

12. See Emmanuel Ghent, "Masochism, Submission, Surrender:

Masochism as a Perversion of Surrender," *Contemporary Psycho-analysis* 26 (1990): 108–36.

13. Jessica Benjamin, *The Bonds of Love* (New York: Pantheon, 1988), p. 129.

14. Mitchell, *Hope and Dread*, p. 31.

15. Harry Stack Sullivan, "The Data of Psychiatry," in *Clinical Studies in Psychiatry*, ed. Helen Swick Perry, Mary Ladd Gawel, and Martha Gibbon (New York: Norton, 1956), p. 33.

16. Jacques Lacan, *Ecrits: A Selection*, trans. Alan Sheridan (New York: Norton, 1966), p. 2.

17. See Roy Schafer, *A New Language for Psychoanalysis* (New Haven, Conn.: Yale University Press, 1976).

18. Robert A. F. Thurman, *Tsong Khapa's Speech of Gold in the Essence of True Eloquence: Reason and Enlightenment in the Central Philosophy of Tibet* (Princeton, N.J.: Princeton University Press, 1984), p. 131.

19. John Blofeld, *The Zen Teaching of Huang Po: On the Transmission of Mind* (New York: Grove Press, 1958), p. 86.

20. Sigmund Freud, "Analysis Terminable and Interminable," in vol. 23 of *Standard Edition of the Complete Psychological Works of Sigmund Freud,* ed. and trans. James Strachey (London: Hogarth Press and Institute of Psychoanalysis, 1964), p. 235.

PART III. THERAPY

1. Joseph Goldstein and Jack Kornfield, *Seeking the Heart of Wisdom: The Path of Insight Meditation* (Boston: Shambhala, 1987), p. 95.

2. D. W. Winnicott, "The Location of Cultural Experience," in *Playing and Reality* (London: Routledge, 1971), p. 100.

3. Sigmund Freud, "Analysis Terminable and Interminable," in vol. 23 of *Standard Edition of the Complete Psychological Works of Sigmund Freud,* ed. and trans. James Strachey (London: Hogarth Press and Institute of Psychoanalysis, 1964), p. 235.

4. Josef Breuer and Sigmund Freud, "Studies on Hysteria," *Standard Edition,* 2:305.

*   *   *

CHAPTER 8. REMEMBERING

1. Sigmund Freud, "Remembering, Repeating and Working-Through," in vol. 12 of *Standard Edition of the Complete Psychological Works of Sigmund Freud*, ed. and trans. James Strachey (London: Hogarth Press and Institute of Psychoanalysis, 1958), p. 147.
2. D. W. Winnicott, "Fear of Breakdown," *International Review of Psycho-Analysis* 1 (1974): 106.
3. Freud, "Remembering, Repeating and Working-Through," *Standard Edition,* 12:149.
4. Bhadantacariya Buddhaghosa, *Visuddhimagga* (Path of purification), trans. Bhikkhu Nyanamoli, vol. 2 (Berkeley, Calif.: Shambhala, 1976), p. 524.
5. Freud, "Remembering, Repeating and Working-Through," *Standard Edition,* 12:147.
6. Michael Balint, *The Basic Fault: Therapeutic Aspects of Regression* (London: Tavistock, 1968), p. 21.
7. Isadore From, personal communication to the author, 1990.
8. Carl Jung, "Yoga and the West," in *Psychology and Religion: West and East*, vol. 11 of *The Collected Works of C. G. Jung*, trans. R. F. C. Hull, Bollingen Series, no. 20 (New York: Pantheon, 1958), p. 537.
9. Buddhaghosa, *Visuddhimagga*, p. 1.

CHAPTER 9. REPEATING

1. Sigmund Freud, "Remembering, Repeating and Working-Through," in vol. 12 of *Standard Edition of the Complete Psychological Works of Sigmund Freud*, ed. and trans. James Strachey (London: Hogarth Press and Institute of Psychoanalysis, 1958), p. 150.
2. sGam.po.pa, *The Jewel Ornament of Liberation*, trans. Herbert V. Guenther (Berkeley, Calif.: Shambhala, 1971), pp. 216–17.
3. W. R. Bion, *Attention and Interpretation* (New York: Basic Books, 1970), p. 42.
4. Janine Chasseguet-Smirgel, "The Femininity of the Analyst in Professional Practice," *International Journal of Psycho-Analysis* 65 (1984): 171.
5. Sandor Ferenczi, "The Elasticity of Psycho-Analytic Technique,"

in *Final Contributions to the Problems and Methods of Psycho-Analysis* (New York: Basic Books, 1955), p. 98.

6. Otto Fenichel, *Problems of Psychoanalytic Technique* (New York: Psychoanalytic Quarterly, 1941), p. 5.

7. Charlotte Joko Beck, *Everyday Zen: Love and Work*, ed. Steve Smith (San Francisco: HarperSanFrancisco, 1989), p. 71. Emphasis added.

8. Marsha M. Linehan, observation made in the course of panel discussion. "The Buddha Meets the West: Integrating Eastern Psychology and Western Psychotherapy" (panel discussion at the annual conference of the Society for the Exploration of Psychotherapy Integration, Cambridge, Mass., April 1988).

9. Hans Loewald, "On the Therapeutic Action of Psychoanalysis," *International Journal of Psycho-Analysis* 58 (1960): 29.

10. Michael Balint, *The Basic Fault: Therapeutic Aspects of Regression* (London: Tavistock, 1968), p. 183.

11. Freud, "Remembering, Repeating," p. 154.

CHAPTER 10. WORKING THROUGH

1. Sigmund Freud, "Remembering, Repeating and Working-Through," in vol. 12 of *Standard Edition of the Complete Psychological Works of Sigmund Freud*, ed. and trans. James Strachey (London: Hogarth Press and Institute of Psychoanalysis, 1958), p. 155.

2. Ibid., p. 151.

3. Freud, "Beyond the Pleasure Principle," *Standard Edition,* 18:20–21.

4. Adam Phillips, *Winnicott* (Cambridge, Mass.: Harvard University Press, 1988), p. 80.

5. Lewis Aron, "Working through the Past—Working toward the Future," *Contemporary Psychoanalysis* 27 (1991): 81–109.

6. Robert Thurman, "What Does Being a Buddhist Mean to You? Re: When You Speak of Letting Go of the Ego, What Is the 'Ego' That You Are Talking About Letting Go Of?" *Tricycle: The Buddhist Review* 3, no. 1 (1993): 28.

7. Otto Fenichel, *The Psychoanalytic Theory of Neurosis* (New York: Norton, 1945), p. 92.

8. Sigmund Freud, *New Introductory Lectures on Psycho-Analysis*, *Standard Edition*, 22:95.

9. See Aron, "Working through the Past."

10. Erich Fromm, "Psychoanalysis and Zen Buddhism," in *Zen Buddhism and Psychoanalysis*, ed. Erich Fromm, D. T. Suzuki, and Richard De Martino (New York: Harper & Row, 1960), p. 86.

Index

Abnormal ego, 161
Absolutism, 90–91
Achaan Chaa, 79–81, 83
Aggression: estrangement from, 34–36; and Hell Realm, 20, 21–25; redirecting, 216–18
Alcohol use, 95
Alexander, Franz, 2
Ali, Muhammad, 94
Analytic inquiry, 8
Ananda, 40, 63
Andreas-Salome, Lou, 2
Anger, acceptance of, 203–4, 206, 207, 209–10, 216
Animal Realm, 15, 16, 18, 20, 25–28, 50, 51, 221
Annihilationism, 64
Anuruddha, 142–43
Anxiety: acceptance of, 207–9; and bare attention, 116–17; as experience of nonperfection, 86–87; and Hell Realm, 20, 21–25; of meditators, 135–36; as part of human condition, 46–47
Astonishment, 118–19
Attention and Interpretation (Bion), 189

Balint, Michael, 173, 201
Bare attention, 8, 21, 95–96, 109–28, 204, 205, 221; anxiety and, 116–17; astonishment in, 118–19; defined, 110; fearlessness of, 119–21; free association and, 135; impersonality of, 122–25; openness in, 115–17; and power of awareness, 125–26; in psychoanalysis, 113–15, 186–97; suspension of critical faculty in, 114–15; transformational potential of, 111–13
Basic fault, 179–80, 201; acceptance of, 205; Buddhist equivalent of, 211–12; defined, 173–74; evidence of, 193; and repetition, 193, 198, 201; and silence, 186–87
Batchelor, Stephen, 56
Beat poets, 4
Beck, Charlotte Joko, 193
Benjamin, Jessica, 149–50
Bion, W. R., 9, 41, 188–89, 222

Bodhisattva, defined, 16
Bodhisattva of Compassion, 16–17;
    in Animal Realm, 25; in God
    Realm, 31–32; and Hell Realm,
    22; in Realm of the Hungry
    Ghosts, 30; in Realm of the
    Jealous Gods, 34–35, 37
Body, in Right Mindfulness,
    144–45
Bollas, Christopher, 72
Breath, in Right Mindfulness,
    145–47, 168–69
Brown, Daniel, 135–36
Buddha, 7–8; and absolute cer-
    tainty, 62–63; awareness and,
    183; on craving, 59–60, 61–63,
    69; and enlightenment, 43; and
    impersonality of experience,
    125; on importance of mindful-
    ness, 141–42; life story,
    178–79; on meditation, 106; on
    the Middle Path, 137; on narcis-
    sism, 47–48, 69; period of wan-
    dering and teaching, 44; and
    power of "not-knowing," 56;
    raft parable of, 105–6; on the
    self, 47–48, 63–65, 153; on suf-
    fering and humiliation, 43–46;
    vision of Wheel of Life, 40–41.
    See also Four Noble Truths (Bud-
    dha)

Cage, John, 115–16, 118
Campbell, Joseph, 5
Central Way. See Madhyamika school
Chasseguet-Smirgel, Janine, 190
Chinese Buddhism, 7
Civilization and Its Discontents
    (Freud), 2–3
Codependents, 32

Compassion, 83, 175
Concentration, 8, 132, 139–41,
    170, 207, 210, 221
Concretization of experience, 87–88
Confluence, 31–33
Cosmic consciousness, 5
Craving: extinction of, 77–79,
    82–83, 84, 159; in Second
    Noble Truth, 59–60, 61–63,
    69, 76–77, 141, 148–49, 151
Creative activity: bodily expression
    and, 144–45; and Human
    Realm, 37–38; sublimation and,
    78–79, 82
"Critical faculty," suspension of
    (Freud), 114–15

Dalai Lama, 73, 98, 174, 177, 221
Delight, in meditation, 131–33,
    222
Delusion, and the Wheel of Life,
    39–41
De Martino, Richard, 55–56
Desire, of psychotherapist, 189,
    192–93
Dhammapada, 75
Dharma combat, 13–14
Disavowal, of ego, 98–99
Dogen (Zen master), 20
Drama of the Gifted Child, The
    (Miller), 67–68
Drug use, 95

Ego, 70, 92; abnormal, 161; con-
    ventional notions of, 93–94;
    development of, 155; disavowal
    of, 98–99; estrangement from,
    34–36; and instinctual emo-
    tions, 212–13; and meditation,
    94, 132–34; Rank on, 51–52;

split, 134–36, 138; surrender of, 147–51

Ego boundaries, relaxation of, 31–33, 210

Ego libido, 81–82, 83

Eigen, Michael, 33, 118, 146

Eightfold Path, 92, 101–2; Right Action in, 92; Right Concentration in, 92, 132, 139–41; Right Livelihood in, 92; Right Mindfulness in, 92, 95–96, 132, 139–51, 168–69; Right Speech in, 92; Right Thought in, 92; Right Understanding in, 92; Right View in, 92, 99

Emotions: estrangement of, 205–9; holding, 25, 101–2, 221; instinctual, as empty of content, 212–16; and meditation, 92, 101–2; and original unfulfilled needs, 209–12; repression of, 181, 182; sublimation of, 25–26, 78–79, 82, 221–22

Emptiness: basic fault and, 171, 173–74, 198; of Hungry Ghosts, 28–31; and meditation, 90–91, 100–101; and sense of purpose, 222; Western concept of, 19–20, 29–31, 37–38, 64–68, 177–78. See also Sunyata (emptiness)

Enablers, 32

Engler, Jack, 135–36

Enmeshed self, 176–77

Eros, 39, 59–60

Eros myth, 150

Eternalists, 64

False self: Buddhist view of, 92; crumbling of, 73; and identity confusion, 65–68; surrender of, 149, 151; true self versus, 71–73; two poles of, 64; Winnicott on, 37–38, 52–53, 149

Family, eastern versus western sense of, 175–78, 197

Fearlessness, 119–21

"Fear of life" (Rank), 52

Femininity: fear of, 190; and self-esteem, 97

Fenichel, Otto, 192

Ferenczi, Sandor, 2, 192

Four Noble Truths (Buddha): First Truth (humiliation and suffering), 43–47, 55–57; Second Truth (craving), 59–60, 61–63, 69, 76–77, 141, 148–49, 151; Third Truth (extinction of craving), 77–79, 82–83, 84, 159; Fourth Truth (Middle Path), 64, 91–92, 94, 99, 100–102, 137

Free association, 135, 164–65, 166–67, 170–71, 179, 193

Freud, Sigmund, 2–3, 4, 7, 8, 9, 39, 49, 118, 125, 179; and Animal Realm, 18, 20; on ego development, 155; and evenly suspended attention in psychoanalysis, 113–15, 192; on illness, 17; on the instincts, 213; and meditation, 106–7; and narcissism, 48, 49–51, 53–54; and "oceanic experiences," 33, 95, 122, 139, 222; pleasure principle, 60–61, 69, 81–82, 109–10; and remembering in psychotherapy, 163–67, 178–80; and repetition, 181, 183, 189–90, 198, 201–2; on sexuality, 25–26; on sublima-

Freud, Sigmund *(continued)*
    tion, 78–79; on successful ther-
    apy, 160–61; on suffering,
    49–51; on wish fulfillment, 85,
    87; and working through, 204
From, Isadore, 175–76
Fromm, Erich, 4, 221–22

God Realm, 15, 16, 18, 20, 31–33,
    51
Goldstein, Joseph, 107, 113, 149
Goleman, Daniel, 138
"Good enough mother" (Winni-
    cott), 24–25, 118, 177
Grandiosity, 64–65
Great Doubt, 96
Greed, 79; and the Wheel of Life,
    39–41
Guenther, Herbert, 100–101

Hakuin (Zen master), 72–73
Hate, 24–25
Hatred, 79; and the Wheel of Life,
    39–41
Healthy narcissism, 69
Hell Realm, 15, 16, 20, 21–25,
    206
Holding emotions, 25, 101–2, 221
Hopkins, Jeffrey, 174
Horney, Karen, 4
Huang Po, 155
Hui-neng (Zen patriarch), 87,
    90–91
Human Realm, 15–16, 18, 20–21,
    36–38, 179
Humiliation: in First Noble Truth,
    43–47, 55–57; inevitability of,
    44–45
Humility, and narcissism, 45
Hunger, and Animal Realm, 25–28

Hung-jen (Zen patriarch), 89–91
Hungry Ghosts, Realm of, 15, 18,
    28–31, 171, 174, 177, 179,
    210, 221
Huxley, Aldous, 5
Hypnosis, 163–64, 166–67, 179

"I," sense of, 152–53, 209–12,
    216–18, 219, 220, 221
Id, 40, 207
Idealization, 150
Identity, 18
Identity confusion, 5–6, 52, 152;
    and false self, 65–68
Ignorance, 79, 87–88
Impersonality, of bare attention,
    122–25
Infantile helplessness, 3
Injured innocence, 211–12, 216,
    220, 222
Insight *(vipassana)* meditation, 152
Instinctual drives, 78, 212–13
Interpretation of Dreams, The (Freud), 2
Isolation, as defensive posture,
    19–20

James, William, 1–2, 3, 5, 6, 9
Jealous Gods, Realm of, 15, 16,
    34–36
Jewish sobriety (Freud), 2, 3, 9
Jones, Ernest, 2
Jung, Carl G., 2, 4, 5, 176, 178

Kalu Rinpoche, 13–14, 101
Karma (merit), 16
King of Samadhi Scripture, 153
Kipling, Rudyard, 176
Klein, Melanie, 20
Kohut, Heinz, 20
Kornfield, Jack, 79, 140–41

Lacan, Jacques, 152
Laing, R. D., 119
Lankavatara Sutra, 40, 71
Libido, 81; ego, 81–82, 83; foundation of, 81–82; object, 81–82, 83
Linehan, Marsha M., 194
Loewald, Hans, 200–201
Love: estrangement from, 170–72; lack of, 49, 51–52; and lost state of perfection, 85–87
Love of proportion (Freud), 2, 3, 9
Low self-esteem, 30–31, 177, 179–80

Madhyamika school, 70–71, 73, 90, 100
Mala (wooden rosary), 13–14
Mandala, 15, 16
Maslow, Abraham, 4, 20
Masochism, 97
Meditation, 3–4, 6, 8; ascetic practices in, 137; availability of psyche in, 3; and basic fault, 179–80; beginning stages of, 134–36; as deconstructive, 129; eastern versus western approaches to, 176–80; ego functions necessary for, 94, 132–34; and the Eightfold Path, 92, 101–2; and emotions, 92, 101–2; emptiness and, 100–101; estrangement and, 170–72; and Freud, 106–7; holding emotions in, 101–2; insight in, 151–55; narcissism in, 133–34; pain in, 136–37, 214–16; power of awareness and, 125–26; primitive longing in, 136–37; psy-chotherapy compared with, 107, 129–31, 135–36, 167, 183–84, 220; raft metaphor for, 105–6; remembering and, 167–70, 176–80, 191, 210; and repetition, 201–2; sexual issues in, 27–28; spatial metaphor for self in, 137–41, 207; for stress reduction, 96; terror and delight in, 131–33; as transitional object, 123–25; to withdraw from confusion, 99; working through in, 206–7. *See also* Bare attention
Memory, of psychotherapist, 189, 192–93
Merton, Thomas, 5
Middle Path, 64, 91–92, 137
Miller, Alice, 67–68
Milner, Marion, 144–45
Mindfulness, 8, 95–96, 132, 141–51, 166
Mitchell, Stephen A., 138, 143
"Muscular armoring" (Reich), 51

Nagarjuna (Buddhist scholar), 70–71, 90, 100
Narcissism, 3, 4, 6, 7, 18, 20, 39, 150; Buddha on, 47–48, 69; elimination of, 41; and Freud, 48, 49–51, 53–54; and Human Realm, 37–38; and humility, 45; and meditative practice, 133–34; pathological versus healthy, 69; penetration of, 45; primary, 81, 87; relativity of, 210–11
Narcissistic craving, 59–60
Narcissistic dilemma, 6
Narcissus myth, 21, 47, 48

Nasruddin, story of, 159–60
Neglect, 173–74
New Introductory Lectures (Freud), 213
Nihilism, 90–91
Nirvana, 18, 40, 71, 83
Nonverbal communication, 190

Objectification, 150
Object libido, 81–82, 83
Object relations (Winnicott), 25, 39
"Oceanic" experiences (Freud), 33, 95, 122, 139, 222
On Kissing, Tickling, and Being Bored (Phillips), 70
Openness, in bare attention, 115–17
Oral rage, 172, 199
Organismic potency (Reich), 93
Orgasm: and Animal Realm, 27; genital vs. ego (Rank), 51–52; and God Realm, 31, 32; and Realm of the Hungry Ghosts, 29. *See also* Sexuality

Padma Sambhava, 23
Pain, in meditation, 136–37, 214–16
Pathological narcissism, 69
Peak experiences, 31
Philistine timidity (Freud), 2, 3, 9
Phillips, Adam, 70
Phobias, 21–23
Pleasure principle (Freud), 60–61, 69; foundation of, 81–82; and mental processes, 109–10
"Primal scream," 93–94
Primary narcissism, 81, 87
Problem of Psychoanalytic Technique, The (Fenichel), 192
Pseudonirvana, 150–51

Psyche: availability of, in meditation, 3; unresolved material in, 188
Psychedelia, 4
Psyche myth, 149–50
Psychoanalysis, 2, 4–5, 7; bare attention in, 113–15, 186–97; evolution of, 39, 49–53; instinctual drives in, 78
Psychotherapist: analytic attitude of, 182; desire of, 189, 192–93; memory of, 189, 192–93
Psychotherapy: false self in, 71–73; and identity confusion, 65–68; integration of Buddha's teaching into, 8–9; meditation compared with, 107, 129–31, 135–36, 167, 183–84, 220; as reconstructive, 129; remembering in, 163–67, 178–80; resistance in, 121, 165, 182–83; self in, 151–53; suffering in, 49–53; termination of, 218–20; transference in, 129–31, 182, 184–86; true self in, 71–73

Rank, Otto, 2, 51–52
Reality principle (Freud), 60–61, 69
Realm of the *Asuras* (Jealous Gods or Titans), 15, 16, 34–36
Realm of the *Pretas* (Hungry Ghosts), 15, 18, 28–31, 171, 174, 177, 179, 210, 221
Reich, Annie, 97
Reich, Wilhelm, 19, 49, 51, 93
Remembering, 163–80; Freud on, 163–67, 178–80; of trauma, 167–70, 191, 210
Reparation, 195, 197–200, 216
Repetition, 181–202, 210; atten-

tion to, in psychotherapy, 183, 193–97, 204; and basic fault, 193, 198, 201; and desire of therapist, 189, 192–93; Freud and, 181, 183, 189–90, 198, 201–2; and memory of therapist, 189, 192–93; noninterference and, 189–91; and reparation, 195, 197–200, 216; and repression of memories, 181, 182; silence and, 184–89, 190, 191; transference and, 182, 184–86

Repression, 181, 182

Resistance, in psychotherapy, 121, 165, 182–83

Ridgepole of ignorance, 76–77

Right Action, 92

Right Concentration, 92, 132, 139–41

Right Livelihood, 92

Right Mindfulness, 92, 95–96, 132, 141–51; body in, 144–45; breath in, 145–47, 168–69; surrender in, 147–51; time in, 142–44

Right Speech, 92

Right Thought, 92

Right Understanding, 92

Right View, 92, 99

Rogers, Carl, 20

Rolland, Romain, 2–3

Samsara. See Wheel of Life (Wheel of Samsara)

Samyutta Nikaya (Kindred Sayings), 106

Schiller, Friedrich von, 106

Self, 92; awareness of, 5–6; Buddha on, 47–48; in Buddhism, 63–65, 70–73, 87–88; and Human Realm, 36–38; insight and, 151–55; instincts and, 213–14; as metaphor, 154–55; as purposive agent, 76; spatial metaphor for, 137–41, 207

Self-esteem: and femininity, 97; low, 30–31, 177, 179–80

Selflessness, 201; as disavowal of ego, 98–99; organismic potency versus, 93–94; as subjugation of emotion, 96–97; as union, 94–96

Self-sufficiency: absence of, 100; "False Self" as form of, 53; illusion of, 44, 48, 154

Seng-tsan (Zen patriarch), 86

Separation, and transitional objects, 122–24

Separation anxiety, 52

Setting in Motion the Wheel of Truth (Dhammacakkappavattana Sutra), 45–46

Seung Sahn, 13

Sexuality: and Animal Realm, 25–28, 50; frustrated anger in, 49–51. See also Orgasm

Shen-hsiu, 90–91

Silence, 184–89; in darshan, 185–86; in psychotherapy, 186–89; and repetition, 184–89, 190, 191; and sunyata, 190, 191

Six Realms of Existence, 15, 106; Animal Realm, 15, 16, 18, 20, 25–28, 50, 51, 221; God Realm, 15, 16, 18, 20, 31–33, 51; Hell Realm, 15, 16, 20, 21–25, 206; Human Realm, 15–16, 18, 20–21, 36–38, 179;

Six Realms of Existence *(continued)*
    Realm of the *Asuras* (Jealous
    Gods or Titans), 15, 16, 34–36;
    Realm of the *Pretas* (Hungry
    Ghosts), 15, 18, 28–31, 171,
    174, 177, 179, 210, 221
Sogyal Rinpoche, 176, 177
Somatization, 165
Spatial metaphors, 137–41, 207
Split ego, 134–36, 138
Stress reduction, 96, 119–20
Subjugation, of emotion, 96–97
Sublimation, 25–26, 221–22; and
    creative activity, 78–79, 82
Suffering: in First Noble Truth,
    43–47, 55–57; inevitability of,
    44–45; and psychotherapy,
    49–53
Sullivan, Harry Stack, 152
Sunyata (emptiness), 72; described,
    38, 100–101; origins of term,
    190. *See also* Emptiness
Suppressed Madness of Sane Men, The
    (Milner), 144–45
Surrender, in Right Mindfulness,
    147–51
Suzuki Roshi, 127

Takasui (Zen master), 56–57
Tantric meditation practices, 28, 83
Taoism, 7
Termination, of psychotherapy,
    218–20
Terror, in meditation, 131–33, 222
Thanatos, 39
Thurman, Robert, 99, 211
*Tibetan Book of Living and Dying,
    The* (Sogyal Rinpoche), 176
Tibetan Buddhism, 174–75, 211

Time, in Right Mindfulness,
    142–44
Tranquility of mind, 150, 175
Transference, 129–31; defined,
    182; and repetition, 182,
    184–86
Transitional objects, 122–25
"Transitional space" (Winnicott),
    122, 124, 126
Trauma, remembering, 167–70,
    191, 210
True self, 39, 111; Buddhist
    approach to, 65–66, 71–73;
    false self versus, 71–73; Winni-
    cott on, 72
Tsong Khapa, 153
"Two sicknesses" (Buddhism),
    50–51

Union, selflessness as, 94–96

Vinci, Leonardo da, 78–79
Visuddhimagga (Path of purifica-
    tion), 131–32

Watts, Alan, 5
Wheel of Life (Wheel of Samsara),
    15–18, 20, 39, 154, 204; Bud-
    dha's vision of, 40–41, 106
Winnicott, D. W., 20, 24–25, 160,
    165; on False Self, 37–38,
    52–53, 149; on openness, 115,
    117; on True Self, 72
Wisdom, 83
Working-through, 160, 203–18

Zen, 7, 89, 211
Zen Buddhism and Psychoanalysis,
    55–56, 221–22